Haunted Holidays

Haunted Holidays

Twelve Months of Kentucky Ghosts

Roberta Simpson Brown
and Lonnie E. Brown

Scholarly publisher for the Commonwealth,
serving Bellarmine University, Berea College, Centre
College of Kentucky, Eastern Kentucky University,
The Filson Historical Society, Georgetown College,
Kentucky Historical Society, Kentucky State University,
Morehead State University, Murray State University,
Northern Kentucky University, Transylvania University,
University of Kentucky, University of Louisville,
and Western Kentucky University.

Editorial and Sales Offices: The University Press of Kentucky
663 South Limestone Street, Lexington, Kentucky 40508-4008
www.kentuckypress.com

Library of Congress Cataloging-in-Publication Data

Brown, Roberta Simpson, 1939-
Haunted holidays : twelve months of Kentucky ghosts / Roberta Simpson Brown and Lonnie E. Brown.
pages cm
ISBN 978-0-8131-6555-4 (pbk. : alk. paper) — ISBN 978-0-8131-6570-7 (pdf) — ISBN 978-0-8131-6569-1 (epub) 1. Ghosts—Kentucky. 2. Haunted places—Kentucky. 3. Holidays—Miscellanea. I. Title.
BF1472.U6B765 2015
133.109769--dc23

2015011471

This book is printed on acid-free paper meeting
the requirements of the American National Standard
for Permanence in Paper for Printed Library Materials.

Manufactured in the United States of America.

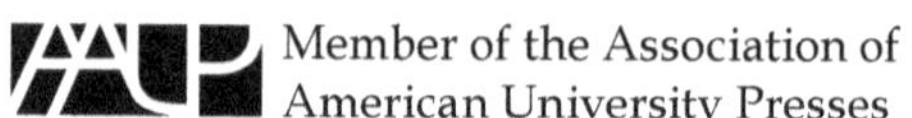

To Dwayne VanderEspt and Jerry Anderson

Contents

Introduction

This collection of stories was inspired by the strangest request for a story that we have ever had. It came from the ghost of a young boy! We were amazed at the way it happened.

At the start of Memorial Day weekend on May 24, 2013, we joined our friend Sharon Brown on a tour of Wickland, a haunted historic mansion in Bardstown, Kentucky. The historic aspect of the mansion alone would be of sufficient interest to draw people to take a tour; however, the presence of ghostly spirits in the mansion adds its own magic.

Built between 1825 and 1828, Wickland was the home of three governors.

Its first owner was Charles Anderson Wickliffe, who was governor from 1839 to 1840, having assumed office when Governor James Clark died in office in 1839. Charles Wickliffe's son, Robert C. Wickliffe, served as governor from 1856 to 1860. Later, after Governor William Goebel's assassination in 1900, Charles Wickliffe's grandson, John Crepps Wickliffe Beckham, became governor and, after a special election, served until 1907. All three governors from the Wickliffe family made Wickland their home at some point during their lives.

After a succession of owners after 1919, the Nelson County Fiscal Court purchased Wickland in 2003. In 2004 the nonprofit organization Friends of Wickland opened the house for tours and activities.

There were more than twenty people on the tour we took on May 24, 2013. We knew none of them except our friend Sharon Brown, and none of them knew us. The tour was conducted by the manager of Wickland, Dixie Hibbs, and a medium. (You may call Dixie at 502-507-0808 for more information about the house or reservations for a tour.) The medium used dowsing rods to help us communicate with the Wickland spirits. There are a number of spirits in the house, and no one can predict which ones will show up.

According to Dixie, the strongest spirit in Wickland is Waleta, a large black woman who did the cooking at the house. Waleta shares colorful details of life at Wickland and answers questions from those on the tour. The day we visited, we encountered her spirit through the medium in the kitchen. At least on that day, Waleta seemed especially concerned with the weather. Although we found her comments interesting and entertaining, she said nothing that we could check on as being true.

We ended the tour in the basement of the house, where a young slave boy was said to appear at times. Sure enough, on this night, he was there. All of us sat in a circle, and the medium stood behind the chair of each of us, one at a time. She would hand the dowsing rods to the individual she was standing behind and let the little boy give each person a message. Since there were over twenty of us, the process took quite a while. The medium finally stood behind our friend Sharon, who passed the rods on to Lonnie without waiting for a message. All three of us had already had experience using dowsing rods, and Sharon wanted to allow more time for the others in the large circle. Lonnie turned to Roberta, and, as he held out the rods and Roberta reached for them, the young boy's voice spoke clearly through the medium.

"Tell me a story!" he said.

Sharon and the two of us gasped and then started laughing at the same time. The others in the room looked puzzled and asked what was going on.

We said to the group, "We're professional storytellers!"

Nobody except Sharon knew that, so there was no way the medium could have faked the spirit's request! We wished that we could have told him a story then and there, but the session had to continue. It was so inspiring to have contact with a spirit at Memorial Day, a time when we remember the dead and celebrate their lives.

The spirit's request stayed in our minds. We remember the times we sat with relatives and friends and told stories, especially during the Christmas holidays. (As you may know, Christmas used to be the traditional time for telling ghost stories, not Halloween.) We know some of the stories are true because we experienced them firsthand. Some we believe because we heard them from family and friends.

If we have left out a holiday in this collection, it is because we do not yet have a story related to it; however, we are always looking for new stories.

So, Young Ghost Boy of Wickland, as well as all the story lovers who have gone before and all on this side who appreciate a spooky tale, these stories are for you!

Martin Luther King Jr. Day

Martin Luther King Jr., clergyman and nonviolent activist for the civil rights movement, was born on January 15, 1929, in Atlanta, Georgia. He died by an assassin's bullet in Memphis, Tennessee, on April 4, 1968.

We celebrate Martin Luther King Jr. Day on the third Monday in January. Although originally intended to commemorate King's birthday, the holiday, like other holidays set under the Uniform Monday Holiday Act, always falls on a Monday. It was officially observed in all fifty states for the first time in the year 2000.

Dr. King was a leader of the civil rights movement in the 1950s and 1960s and led marches and demonstrations for social justice. He was a complex person and, like everyone, had his flaws, but is a hero to those seeking freedom in a nonviolent way.

Little Martin

A nurse friend of ours told us this story. She asked that we not use her full name or the name of the Kentucky hospital where she worked because the hospital did not like nurses telling stories about their patients.

Lula worked in a ward for the terminally ill. One patient captured her heart the minute he was brought in.

Martin was ten years old and was dying of cancer. He had undergone surgery, chemo treatments, and radiation, but the cancer had spread through his small body anyway. Now he was simply waiting to die.

There was no denial about his condition. His parents had talked to him and tried to answer his questions about death the best they could. Martin had accepted his coming death.

Lula learned the name of the little boy's hero right away, because he carried a book about Dr. Martin Luther King Jr.

"I am named after him, you know," Martin told Lula. "I am glad Momma liked him, so she would name me Martin. Don't you think that's a good name?"

"I do, indeed," Lula told him.

As the days passed, Martin fought to live with courage. The medication eased the pain somewhat, but Martin asked to have only what he needed. He wanted to be awake to read and talk to people.

"I wish I could have met Dr. King," said Martin. "Do you think I'll meet him on the other side after I die?"

"Maybe so," Lula told him. "I am sure he would have liked to meet you."

Martin read from his book every day, and each day he looked weaker than the day before. He still managed a smile when Lula or his parents came into the room. He never complained about the terrible disease that had imprisoned him.

One night Lula came on duty to find that Martin was very restless. She had to spend quite a bit of time with him that night until he finally drifted off to sleep in the wee hours of morning. About three hours before her shift ended, she went in to check on him and found him calm and wide awake.

"How are you feeling?" she asked Martin.

"I had the best dream ever!" he told her. "I dreamed Dr. King came to visit me!"

"That is a great dream," Lula said. "Did he say anything?"

"He said he'll be with me the rest of tonight and that he'll see me when I wake up in the morning," said Martin.

"That's nice," said Lula, tucking him in. "Now try to get some rest."

"He said tomorrow will be a special day," said Martin, closing his eyes and drifting off.

Lula finished her rounds and was heading to the desk to check out when she noticed a flurry of activity in Martin's room. She hurried in as another nurse pulled the sheet over Martin's face. She was crying, and Lula started to cry, too.

"He went so peacefully," the nurse said. "And look what I found under his covers."

She held up a picture of Dr. King.

"I never saw this before," she said. "Did you?"

"No," said Lula. "I only saw his book."

Had Martin been dreaming or had it been real? she wondered.

She looked at the calendar on the wall by Martin's bed. The day was January 15. It was the day Dr. King had been born and the day little Martin had died. Had the two finally met?

Lula punched out and left for home. The sweet smile on little Martin's face stayed with her for a long time. He'd had a dream like Dr. King, and now they both were "free at last."

Valentine's Day

Valentine's Day (also known as St. Valentine's Day or the Feast of St. Valentine) is celebrated February 14, a date fixed by the Catholic Church.

It is said that St. Valentine of Rome sent the first valentine. He was imprisoned for performing weddings for soldiers who were forbidden to marry and for ministering to Christians. Legend states that, while imprisoned, he healed his jailer's daughter. It is also said that, before his execution, he wrote her a farewell letter and signed it "Your Valentine."

This holiday began as a liturgical celebration of early Christian saints named Valentine. It was first associated with romantic love by Geoffrey Chaucer in the High Middle Ages, when courtly love flourished.

In the eighteenth century in England, Valentine's Day evolved into a day when lovers sent greeting cards, candy, and flowers to express their love for each other.

Since the nineteenth century, store-bought cards have replaced handwritten valentines.

Valentine symbols today include heart shapes, doves, and Cupid figures.

This day reminds us that love is stronger than death, and ghosts can return to pay us a visit.

The Phantom Bells

According to the stories passed on from Roberta's grandmother, Fanny Dean, to Roberta's mother, Lillian Dean Simpson, phantom bells offer guidance for passing between life and death. Grandma Fanny passed on one story concerning phantom bells.

When she was a little girl, Lillian had one question that bothered her, so she asked her mother about it.

"Mom, with so many dead people on the other side, how will we find the ones we love when we die?" she asked.

"I have heard that phantom bells will guide us," said Grandma Fanny.

"I don't hear any bells when people die," said little Lillian. "The church bell doesn't ring because somebody stole the clapper."

"Phantom bells are not church bells," said Grandma Fanny. "Only the dead can hear them."

Lillian dropped the subject. She didn't want to think about dead people hearing bells.

She wanted to think only of the living. Lillian's neighbor, Bradley, and his girlfriend, Bernice, were going to be married on Valentine's Day, and the whole neighborhood was invited.

Social events out in the country were important to people who didn't have too many things to celebrate publicly.

Lillian hoped that whoever took the clapper would return it by the wedding. It wasn't a very funny prank, she thought.

A week before Valentine's Day, Bradley was coming home with a wagon filled with supplies for his farm. Nobody was with him, so nobody knew what really happened as he headed home. Something must have spooked his horse and overturned the wagon. Bradley's neck was broken, and he died.

Bernice was shattered by the news. Her wedding day would now be spent at Bradley's funeral. She cried and cried. No one could console her.

Valentine's Day arrived. Everyone in the community gathered at the little church to say good-bye to Bradley. The crowd was large, for Bradley had been well liked. It was a cloudy winter day. The corner of the graveyard where Bradley was being laid to rest was gloomy.

The preacher read from the Bible and preached his sermon of everlasting life. As they sang "When They Ring Those Golden Bells for You and Me," the mourners filed by for a last look and proceeded to the graveside to wait for all the others to join them.

Bradley's coffin was lowered into the grave; all bowed their heads in silent prayer. Suddenly Bernice ran forward, sobbing, and threw herself down on the coffin. Those who rushed to help her out stepped back in amazement. The preacher checked her pulse.

"She's dead," the preacher announced to those gathered.

As they stood in stunned silence, the sun burst through the clouds as if the whole sky had lit up!

At that moment, Lillian happened to look up at the bell tower of the church. It was swinging wildly in silent celebration. Lillian knew Bradley and Bernice had found each other on the other side.

Love Never Dies

When we lived near the Smith Woods in Adair County, we heard spooky stories from our neighbors all year round. An especially haunting story is set at Valentine's Day.

Though we associate Valentine's Day with love and gifts and happiness, the holiday can be a sad time for those who are alone or who have lost loved ones. We learned that there were star-crossed lovers even in the Smith Woods. Lonnie's mother, Lena, heard this story and passed it on to him.

Two families lived on opposite sides of the woods. They had been at odds with each other for years over a boundary line, and the dispute eventually grew into a full-fledged feud. Though it never reached the magnitude of the Hatfields and the McCoys' feud, it was just as deadly. Quite some time had passed since the last outbreak between the families, and in that time, the young girl in one family and the young man in the other fell in love, just like Romeo and Juliet.

And just like the two doomed lovers that Shakespeare wrote about, these two young people met with strong opposition from their families. The young lovers chose to ignore the protests. So the feud heated up again. Each family was determined to keep the two apart.

The young couple sneaked out and met in the woods. They decided that they would elope on Valentine's Day. It was the most romantic thing they could think of. They thought that surely their families would accept their marriage once it was legally done.

They decided that the girl should pack her bag and have it ready. Then, on February 14, at midnight, when all were asleep except them, they would put their plan into action.

The young man would come on horseback through the woods and pick up his beloved. Then they would ride into town to be married.

That night, the girl was ready. All were asleep, or so she thought. She listened by the window and she heard the rider and horse approaching through the woods. She didn't know that her father heard the rider, too.

When the girl slipped to the door to go out to meet her loved one, her father came quietly behind her with his gun.

"Get back to your room right now!" he ordered.

He opened the door and stepped outside with the gun.

"No, Daddy! No!" she screamed.

Her father yelled into the darkness. "Get back and get on home if you want to live," he called. "I know what you're up to."

"No!" the young man yelled back. "I love your daughter and I'm going to marry her!"

The young man continued to ride toward the house.

"Halt or I'll shoot!" yelled the father, but the young man kept coming.

A shot rang out. The horse whinnied and reared in the air. The young girl screamed, and the young man fell dead to the ground. In the morning, members of the boy's family came to claim their own and execute revenge.

It was said that the young girl died of a broken heart soon afterward. And people swore that year after year, they could hear a horse and rider coming through the woods at midnight on Valentine's Day. A ghostly figure of a young girl would appear in the window, waiting for her beloved.

The Smith Woods are gone today. The trees were cut down and replaced by subdivisions. The beautiful spot by the waterfall was changed forever and the woods were never the same.

We wonder if the people living in those subdivisions ever hear a ghostly rider in the night on Valentine's Day, or if they see a ghostly young lady looking into woods that are no longer there. If they do, then they must know that love never dies.

Lily Rose Is Still Screaming

Aunt Lily Simpson passed this story down through Roberta's family because she liked the name Lily Rose. Other than sharing the name, however, Aunt Lily didn't want to be like the girl in the story.

Ladies in Kentucky were often named after flowers. The

names Lily, Rose, Daisy, Pansy, and Violet, for example, were common. Sometimes two names were combined, like Lily Rose.

The Lily Rose that Roberta's Aunt Lily remembered was a young woman in the Appalachian area near the Tennessee state line. She was the only girl in a large family, and her chores took up most of her waking hours.

She had to cook breakfast for her brothers and parents, wash dishes, sweep the floors, make the beds, slop the hogs, feed the chickens, wash the family's clothes on Monday (the traditional laundry day), iron, cook the noon meal, and do other jobs that seemed to pop up endlessly during the day.

Of course, Lily Rose was not the only one in the family who worked. Her mother tended the garden, and her father and brothers did the other work on the farm. She understood that it took everybody to make a living for the family, but she longed for a better life, with her own home and someone to love her.

Because the family lived far away from town, it seemed unlikely that Lily Rose would ever meet anyone to fulfill her dreams; but then it happened.

A new minister arrived that fall to serve at the little country church where Lily Rose lived. He was handsome, kind, and, best of all, he was a widower! His wife had died three years before of scarlet fever, and they had never had children. He and Lily Rose hit it off from the start.

The young preacher came to call every Sunday after church services and had dinner with the family, but the relationship didn't proceed as fast as Lily Rose would have liked. One day she blurted out her concerns.

"I thought you cared for me," she said.

"I do," he told her. "But the truth is, I don't know if I dare marry you or not."

"What do you mean?" she asked. "Why shouldn't we get married if we care about each other?"

"I haven't told you much about my late wife," he said. "I know it is wrong to speak ill of the dead, but she was a very jealous woman. When she died, she swore that no other woman would ever have me. I didn't think much about her threat at the time.

"A year after my wife died, I started courting a young lady who was a member of my church. Things began to turn serious, and then one day the lady suddenly refused to see me without an explanation. Of course I persisted until she told me why she didn't want to see me anymore.

"Every night she would have a vivid dream of my dead wife. The face in the dream was horrible, and every night, it would get closer and closer. She told me that she knew if it came again, it would kill her! So she never saw me again.

"I thought it was nonsense, but when I came here and met you, I began to feel my dead wife's presence in the parsonage. I know she isn't really there, but she comes vividly to my mind. I know it sounds crazy, but I am afraid!"

Lily Rose thought about the drudgery that filled her life, and she thought of the wonderful new life she could have as the reverend's wife. She studied a picture of the dead woman and thought that the woman didn't look too menacing. Lily Rose made up her mind that no ghost was going to keep her from her dream.

The preacher and Lily Rose married on Valentine's Day that year. The wedding was everything Lily Rose had ever dreamed of—at least, up to that point.

As soon as Lily Rose moved into the parsonage with her new husband, her dreams began to change. Every night, the dead woman appeared in a dream, and Lily Rose would wake up screaming.

"Her face is hideous!" Lily Rose told her husband. "She is filled with hate, and I can feel her directing it toward me!"

"Maybe you are having the dreams because of what I told you," her husband said. "Maybe that is influencing you to have the nightmares."

Whatever the cause, the dreams kept coming. Lily Rose began to dread bedtime. Now she hardly slept at all for fear she would see that horrible face.

Then came the night that the ghostly figure stood at the foot of the bed. Lily Rose sat up, screaming.

"She was here in this room!" she cried when her husband tried to comfort her. "It wasn't a dream. She is not in the dream anymore. She is here with us!"

"Honey, that's impossible," he said. "Let's pray about it. You will feel better in the morning."

Together they prayed, but in the morning Lily Rose did not feel better. A sense of foreboding filled her whole being. Something bad was going to happen.

That morning, the reverend had to make a house call on one of the parishioners who was ill.

"I'll be home around noon," he told Lily Rose. "Why don't you try to take a nap while I'm gone?"

Lily Rose fought the idea of sleep. She wanted to stay awake, but she had slept little the night before. She had a splitting headache from lack of sleep, so she decided to take an aspirin and lie down to see if it would ease off.

She only intended to rest, but she was soon fast asleep.

The preacher, worried about his wife, hurried to make his call and return home. As he neared the parsonage, he heard Lily Rose screaming. The screams seemed to be torn from her throat. He had never heard such terror.

He ran to the house and flung open the door. Lily Rose was writhing on the bed, struggling with something he could not see. Her efforts seemed to be getting weaker and weaker.

He ran to the bed and raised her up in his arms. She put her hands to her neck, and one last scream died in her throat.

"What's wrong, Lily Rose?" he asked. "Tell me!"

"She came," Lily Rose said in a whisper. "She took my breath . . ."

And with those words, Lily Rose was gone.

There was no official cause of death. People disregarded what the reverend said and decided among themselves that Lily Rose must have choked on something.

The preacher asked to be transferred to another church, and the transfer was granted. The memories were too painful for him to stay on after Lily Rose died.

A new married minister came with his family and settled in the parsonage that spring. All went well through the spring, summer, and fall. Christmas came, and the community worshiped together in the little country church. The young people in the congregation presented a pageant about the birth of Jesus, and the choir sang all the traditional Christmas carols. People felt at peace again and put Lily Rose out of their thoughts.

When they celebrated the New Year, all were certain that it would be a good year. The new minister liked to have as many activities as possible to bring his congregation together, so he planned a Celebration of Love for Valentine's Day.

His plan was to have an old-time meeting and dinner in the church instead of on the grounds outside, since it was cold. Those attending were to bring a fancy packed-box supper to share after the service. Everyone thought it was a wonderful idea, and they gathered at the church next to the parsonage for the noon celebration.

The sermon was beautiful. The minister spoke of love, and everyone quietly listened.

Suddenly the mood was shattered by ear-piercing screams coming from the parsonage.

The screams grew louder and louder and more frantic. Those in the church thought someone must have wandered into the parsonage and was being attacked by something.

The pastor and several of the men ran next door to the parsonage to help whoever was in such distress, but they found no one there. The screams continued for several minutes, then grew weaker and stopped.

By then, the rest of the congregation had come into the churchyard. They stood shivering, not from the cold, but from their memories of Lily Rose and how she died.

For as long as Aunt Lily knew, the screams were heard at noon on every Valentine's Day. Roberta's Aunt Lily has been dead a long, long time; but when we think of her, we think of this story and wonder if Lily Rose is still screaming.

St. Patrick's Day

St. Patrick's Day (in Ireland, the Feast of St. Patrick) is a cultural and religious holiday celebrated each year on March 17, the day St. Patrick died. It is celebrated by the Irish people and people of Irish descent.

The holiday is observed by attending church services, enjoying parades, sporting shamrocks, wearing green, and drinking Irish beer and Irish whiskey. Those who do not drink alcohol might eat Irish potatoes, Irish stew, and Irish soda bread.

Information about St. Patrick comes from the *Declaration,* a letter said to have been written by St. Patrick himself.

Patrick was born in Roman Britain around the fifth century AD, into a wealthy family. It is said that when he was sixteen he was kidnapped by Irish raiders and held as a slave. He worked as a shepherd for six years, and then he found God, who sent him to the coast, where a ship took him on. He became a priest and returned to Ireland to convert the pagan Irish to Christianity.

He is Ireland's most famous saint.

The Irish are known for their legends and tales. Here are some of our favorites.

Menacing March

Lonnie recalls a story he heard from his aunt, Mary Brown.

The month of March was memorable to me as a child for its blustery winds and menacing clouds. It was a time when we kept a close eye on the sky for tornadoes, too. We could see the storms coming in daylight and take proper precautions, but nighttime was another matter. Since we had no weather forecasts, storms sometimes surprised us in the middle of the night.

One good thing about stormy nights when the clouds came up just before bedtime was the storytelling as we sat inside by the fire, the howling wind, booming thunder, and eerie lightning streaks providing colorful special effects. The rain would tap mercilessly on tin roofs and send shivers up our spines.

We were especially lucky if a special storyteller came to visit on such nights to draw our thoughts away from what was going on outside.

Aunt Mary Brown was one of those special storytellers. She carried on the Kentucky tradition of storytelling like few other people could. She was visiting us one night when thunder began to rumble in the west, announcing the coming of dark clouds filled with rain.

We finished supper early. Dad and I took care of the livestock before the storm hit, and we all gathered safely together and asked Aunt Mary to tell us a story.

She said she knew this story to be true because she knew the family involved.

"It happened on a night like this," she said, "only it was one of those storms that sneak up in the night."

Then she told us this story:

The Osborn family lived in a big two-story house that was directly in the path of the storm. After going to the St. Patrick's Day parade, the family members were all sleeping and didn't hear the storm at first.

They had no storm cellar, so they never got up during a storm unless they had left the windows open and the rain was blowing in.

Jack Osborn, age ten, was in his room on the second floor when the thunder woke him. He remembered that he had left the window open because he loved fresh air. He got out of bed and hurried across the floor. He didn't want the rain blowing in and getting things wet.

He looked out the window and saw that the clouds were moving swiftly toward the house. It was a good thing the storm woke him. He reached up to pull the window down quickly, but, as usual, it was stuck.

Jack leaned forward a little and gave the window a strong yank. It didn't budge, but the yank on the window caused him to lose his balance. He grabbed for something to hold on to, but his hands came up empty.

He felt himself falling toward the ground below.

His scream cut through the night, and then, after a thud as he landed, he was deathly still and quiet.

"What was that?" Jack's mother whispered to his father, as she sat up in bed. "It sounded like someone screamed!"

"Must have been the wind shrieking," her husband answered. "It probably blew a limb out of the apple tree."

"You check the windows downstairs," she said. "I'll go up and check on Jack."

They both got out of bed and went to do as Mrs. Osborn had directed. Mr. Osborn went from window to window on the first floor, but they were all closed.

As Mrs. Osborn reached Jack's room, she saw no sign of Jack. She saw the open window, though, and realized what had happened. Oh, no! It couldn't be true! But she knew it was, because she was seeing it with her own eyes.

"Outside! Quick!" she screamed to her husband. "Jack fell out the window!"

They both ran outside, and there on the ground, with his head twisted and his neck definitely broken, lay Jack.

The Osborns stared in disbelief. They stood, stunned, for a moment while the storm raged around them. Then they went inside to call for help.

Two years passed, and the Osborns swore that on stormy nights they would hear Jack's footsteps crossing his old room to close the open window. They never had to worry about rain blowing in during a storm, because Jack's ghost always closed the windows.

"Do you really believe that, Aunt Mary?" I asked her.

"I know now that it's true," she said to me, "but I didn't believe it at first. I thought that Jack's parents were so grief-stricken that they imagined it. However, the next year, I had been to the St. Patrick's Day parade with the Osborns and decided to spend the night at their house, because it was getting too late for me to go home alone.

"I was sleeping in Jack's old room that night when thunder woke me unexpectedly. Mrs. Osborn had left the window open to air out my room, so I knew I needed to close it.

"I sat up in bed and swung my feet to the floor. The air turned cold; and before I could get up, I heard footsteps start at the side of my bed. They crossed the room to the window and stopped. As the rain began to fall, I saw with my own eyes that window close by itself!

"I don't mind telling you that it gave me the chills. I lay back and pulled the covers up around me. I don't think I moved a muscle for the rest of the night. And I never spent another night in that house again."

The Journal

Roberta has always kept a journal, and she is fascinated anytime she comes across an old journal at an estate sale, Goodwill store, thrift store, or yard sale. It is an honor, she feels, when "chance" gives her an opportunity to share the thoughts of another, especially one from long ago.

She tells the following story, which she heard from her Aunt Lily.

On one of their holiday visits, my Uncle Lawrence and Aunt Lily Simpson were sharing stories. Aunt Lily had an intriguing story about a journal she found when she was a young girl.

"We moved to a big house near the Kentucky-Tennessee border when my father was able to get work at a saw mill," she said. "We were surprised that it was in good condition and that the rent was cheap. Best of all, I could have my very own room!

"For two weeks, everything was ideal. We unpacked and settled in by Halloween. We didn't know our neighbors well enough to plan a get-together, but we had homemade treats—pumpkin pies, apples, cookies, and fudge—that my mother made. We all went to bed happy. That was the night the ghost made itself known.

"I remember waking up about 2:00 a.m. to the sound of voices. I thought at first that it was Mom and Dad, but I soon realized that these were the voices of two people I didn't recognize. The woman seemed to be pleading, but the man's voice was angry.

"'Please don't!' the female voice said.

"The male's voice was muffled, but it sounded like he said, 'You're in my way!'

"This was followed by a scuffling sound, then a scream, and the sound of a body rolling down the stairs. There was a thud at the bottom of the stairs and then silence all through the house like nothing had ever happened.

"I got out of bed and opened my door. Mom and Dad had come out of their room, too. It couldn't have been a dream. We all had heard the same thing, but nobody was there. Dad searched the house to make sure no one was hiding, but all was clear. Puzzled, we went back to bed.

"Nothing else happened that night or any night that week. We were beginning to think we had imagined the whole thing, but the wee hours of Sunday morning brought our ghostly visitors again.

"The pleading female voice, the angry male voice, the scuffle, the scream, the body falling down the stairs, and the final thud—all came in the same order as the first time. Again Dad searched the house but found nothing.

"After that, the disturbing event was replayed week after week. It became such a part of our routine that we ignored it. We no longer got out of bed to look around.

"Thanksgiving came and went with the same ghostly performances. Christmas brought a big change, though. The scene was no longer played out for us, but a different kind of haunting took place.

"We were in our living room opening our gifts on Christmas morning when we heard a thud in the hallway. We looked out in the hall and there at the bottom of the steps stood the ghostly woman. She only stayed a couple of seconds and then she was gone.

"In January and February, we heard the thud, but we were so used to it now that we never bothered to look. My parents did ask around about the history of the house, but nobody had any information.

"March was a rainy month that year. One day that month, my parents planned to spend the day helping a neighbor with some work. They asked if I wanted to go, but there was really nothing for me to do there. I decided to stay home. I could have supper ready when they returned.

"The rain and the boredom of being alone inspired me to explore the attic. There was an old trunk up there that we had never looked through. I opened it up and took out the contents, one by one. There were some sheets and pillowcases and a few quilt pieces. A quilt was the last item in the trunk, or so I thought when I lifted it out. That's when I saw the old journal on the bottom.

"My hands were shaking with excitement when I lifted it out and opened it. The text didn't have an introduction. The writer did not say, 'Dear Diary' or anything like that. The writer had just written a partial date followed by an entry. Each entry was signed 'Amanda.'

"The first part of the journal was full of information about daily life. Amanda wrote about her garden, the crops, and her husband's frequent absence from home. Now and then there was a personal entry about her loneliness and her longing to have a child. She began to comment on her husband's change in attitude toward her. He refused to think about having a baby. He refused to take Amanda anywhere, even to town with him on Saturday. The only place she was allowed to go was to church, and she had no time to socialize there. As soon as the service ended, he led her away and went straight home.

"The final entries in the journal took on a more sinister tone. Amanda was suspicious at first. At church, she had heard a whisper about her husband and the young Widow Breeding. Now, when he went away at odd times, she knew he was probably going to Widow Breeding's farm.

"Whenever she tried to talk to her husband about what was going on, he became angry and told her to leave if she didn't like it. She couldn't leave. She had nowhere to go and no skills to work and earn a living for herself.

"One night when he came home about 2:00 a.m., she confronted him about Widow Breeding. He didn't deny it. He told her he was going to divorce her and marry the widow.

"Amanda was frantic. 'I don't know what to do. I can't leave here. I have no family.'

"The last entry in the journal was dated March 17, St. Patrick's Day. *I am afraid my husband is going to kill me and make it look like an accident. What a terrible burden to bear to think that someone who promised to love you forever would be able to take your life! He says I am in the way. Maybe if he kills me, someone will find this journal and know the truth.*

"That was the last thing she wrote. I could hardly wait for my parents to get home so I could show them the journal.

"They were very surprised at the journal's contents. They decided to take it to the local church and let the reverend read it. He checked the church records and found that an Amanda was listed among the members. There was a headstone for her in the graveyard.

"The reverend then did a kind thing. He had a special memorial service for Amanda on St. Patrick's Day, revealing the sad contents of the journal to the congregation.

"I left the journal at the church with the reverend. We stayed on for another year before Dad's job took us elsewhere, but we never saw Amanda's ghost again. I think all she wanted was to have the world hear her side of the story."

Beware of March

Roberta tells this story about her grandmother and their fear of the month of March.

To this day, carry-over fears from my childhood make March a scary month for me. I read in school how Julius Caesar, though warned of his death on the Ides (the 15th) of March by a soothsayer, was murdered on that day. People said that the Ides of March was a day of doom and gloom.

I was afraid of tornadoes and the spring storms that were usually violent in nature. And no child was ever more respectful to fairies and leprechauns on St. Patrick's Day than I was! I wanted to keep a low profile during the entire month so as not to draw bad luck down on my family and me.

Grandmother Simpson reinforced my uneasiness by fearing the month of March herself.

"If I live through March," she would often say, "I'll live another year."

I really worried as a child, because I loved my grandmother very much and I didn't want her to die. I would make a daily check on her to see if she showed any signs of illness. Every year, I breathed a sigh of relief when the Ides of March passed.

"Good!" I'd say to myself. "I'll have Grandma another year!"

Grandmother Simpson was very particular about what she cooked on St. Patrick's Day. She believed corned beef and cabbage were essential to bring good luck. Everyone in the family loved the smell of it all through the house when she was cooking.

When I was about nine years old, we moved away from Grandmother Simpson's farm, and the old lady went to live with her youngest son near Glasgow, Kentucky. Her health was failing, but she still had periods of feeling good enough to come visit. When she would leave, I felt sure I would see her again because she had made it through March.

In 1958, I was a senior in high school. Grandmother Simpson by then was in very poor health, so the family would visit her whenever they could. My uncle kept the family updated about her condition.

Sometimes he would say she was feeling up to having visitors, but we would find when we got there that she had taken a turn for the worse. I hoped the warm weather of spring would make her feel better.

March came, and the days passed as I counted them one by one. The Ides of March went by without incident. Then St. Patrick's Day arrived, and my aunt fixed Grandmother Simpson corned beef and cabbage. It was one of her bad days, so she only ate a few bites. That was a very bad sign. I wished for March to pass and for Grandmother to be all right, but this March, it was not to be. I remembered her words "If I live through March, I'll live another year." She died peacefully on March 21, 1958.

The next year was a hard one. It was not easy to lose Grandmother. The March after her death, I was a freshman at Berea College. On St. Patrick's Day, I thought of her corned beef and cabbage, and sadness washed over me as I realized she was really gone.

I took a walk to try to get my mind off home and all the memories. When I came back to the dorm and opened the door to my room, I was almost overwhelmed by the smell of corned beef and cabbage cooking! I stood there, taking it all in for a moment, and then the smell was gone.

There was a strictly enforced rule about no cooking in the dorm, so I knew it couldn't be anyone really cooking anything. The dorm was located too far from the cafeteria for any cooking odors to drift over. I knew it was a sign from Grandma that I was not alone.

I smiled to myself. I could almost hear Grandmother Simpson saying, "You know, loved ones never leave. I am in another place, but I am not forever gone."

I still remember that on scary days in March.

A St. Patrick's Day Ghost at Waverly?

We never feel a collection of ghost stories is complete without a story about Waverly Hills Sanatorium.

Waverly Hills Sanatorium has often been described as one of the scariest and most haunted places in the world. We have visited the spooky place many times, and something always happens that we can't explain. When we consider the background of Waverly, we are not surprised that this place has truly earned its reputation.

In the 1900s, Louisville, Kentucky, had the highest death rate from tuberculosis in the country. Louisville was such a low valley area that it was the perfect breeding ground for the tuberculosis bacteria. A cruel, brutal lung disease, tuberculosis had no cure at that time. Plenty of rest, fresh air, and nutritious food were the only treatment.

In 1910 a small two-story, forty-bed hospital was built on one of the highest hills in southern Jefferson County to try to contain the disease. It was evident at once that this hospital was not big enough.

Officials began fund-raising for a larger hospital. Soon they had $11 million and land that was donated for the project. Construction was started in 1924, and Waverly Hills opened in 1926 as the most state-of-the-art tuberculosis hospital in the country.

In spite of the dedication of the doctors, nurses, and researchers, however, thousands and thousands of patients died at Waverly. To keep up the morale of those who did have a chance to recover, a "body chute" (or "death tunnel") was built from the hospital to the bottom of the hill, where there were train tracks for trains and vehicles to pick up the dead bodies. The survivors did not have to see the dead carried away.

In 1943 Albert Schatz, a graduate student at Rutgers

University, discovered the antibiotic streptomycin, which pretty much wiped out tuberculosis by the 1950s.

Waverly Hills closed in 1961. It was later reopened as Woodhaven Geriatrics Sanitarium, but the state closed it in 1982 because of the bad treatment it gave its patients.

After that, the land changed hands several times. One owner allowed the building to be almost destroyed by vandals. It is currently owned by Charles and Tina Mattingly, who offer tours that help with the restoration of the building.

With the energy of the life and death of so many people left there, we can understand that paranormal experiences might be commonplace. We strongly urge you to take a tour and see for yourself if you think it is haunted. (You must have reservations, so before you visit, contact Tina Mattingly on Facebook or contact the Waverly Historical Society online.)

We have no identity for the ghost in the following story, but we think it might have been Irish.

A couple from out of town came to visit us one day, and we decided to treat our guests to a ghostly tour of Waverly. During the tour we experienced slamming doors and shadow people, and as we walked by the kitchen, we smelled bread cooking. Our friends were okay with all this, but the lady began to feel a bit spooked as our guide led us down the third-floor hallway.

Our friend dropped to the back of the group when a light showed up in front of us, and then she suddenly called out, "Ouch!"

We all stopped and turned around to see what had happened.

"Which one of you pinched me?" she asked.

"Nobody was behind you," Lonnie pointed out. "None of us pinched you."

"Well, something pinched me," she insisted.

"Maybe it was a ghost," said Roberta.

Our friend did not seem to be too pleased with this suggestion, but she didn't make any more comments at the time.

We all followed our guide a little farther down the hall when again our lady friend called out, "Ouch!"

"Is one of you pulling a prank on me?" she asked. "You are trying to scare me!"

We pointed out again that we were all in front and that she was pinched from behind. She still didn't look convinced.

Nothing further happened until we were almost at the end of the tour. Again the lady interrupted.

"Ouch! That hurt!" she said. "I want to get out of here."

She was happy when we were finally back in our car on our way home.

"Why would something want to pinch me?" she asked.

Her husband laughed and said, "Do you know what day this is?"

"No," she said. "What's that got to do with it?"

"It's St. Patrick's Day!" he told her. "You are the only one wearing brown and orange. The rest of us are wearing green!"

"That's ridiculous," she said. "I never could understand why people get pinched for not wearing green on St. Patrick's Day. It's a silly custom."

Did we have an Irish ghost in our midst that night? Was it just carrying out an old custom? Or was there a presence there that simply did not like our friend?

We have invited the couple to visit and take another tour, but the lady's answer has always been, "I'll think about it."

We have a feeling that, if she does come again, it won't be in March!

Easter

Easter is a religious holiday celebrating the resurrection of Jesus Christ from the dead three days after his crucifixion by the Romans.

The holiday may be observed in several ways—by attending church services or sunrise services, taking part in egg hunts, sharing family meals, and engaging in prayer vigils.

Easter is a movable feast, which means it does not have a fixed day of celebration on the calendar. The earliest direct evidence of the celebration of Easter dates from the middle of the second century AD.

Easter was a special religious holiday to us, as it was to everyone else in our little community. We went to church, sometimes a sunrise service, and prayed in gratitude for Christ's resurrection.

Easter gave us a good feeling because it confirmed our faith in rebirth with the new life of spring. Flowers were blooming, birds were singing, and little animals romped and played.

After church, we came home to eat a big dinner and then have an egg hunt. We didn't have Easter baskets, and the Easter Bunny didn't have us on his list for home delivery. Finding colored eggs and winning small prizes was good enough.

There was only one Easter superstition that we believed in. It was considered good luck to wear new clothes on Easter, so everybody usually showed up at church with new clothes to ensure good fortune during the remainder of the year. It was stylish for ladies to wear new bonnets (usually homemade) and for little girls to wear new black patent leather shoes (which had to be store bought, of course).

Home for Easter

There wasn't much money to spend on our Easter wardrobe, so most of our clothes, especially for females, were homemade. Dresses and shirts were made from feed sacks, sacks that contained food that our fathers bought at the store for the livestock. Flour sacks and sugar sacks were used to make undergarments like panties, slips, and shorts.

Roberta's cousin Emma lived in the city, and she would bring gifts when she came to visit. There were stockings for Roberta's mother and grandmother, pretty anklets for Roberta and her sister, and socks for Roberta's father. Even in the city, Emma knew about the tradition of wearing new clothes on Easter.

One story Emma told about a family she knew in the

Frankfort area always stuck in Roberta's mind. The family was poor, but the father and mother managed to provide new outfits for themselves and their little girl at Easter. The little girl liked brightly colored dresses with white lace collars. She watched her mother sew the new clothes every year and tried to learn how her mom did it.

Then, one year in February, the little girl's mother came down with a fever. Her medicine cost quite a bit of money, and there was little money left when she died. The father barely had enough to provide food, so he told his little daughter that there would be no new clothes for Easter that year.

The weeks passed, and the daughter missed her mother very much. She looked at the sewing machine that she had never learned to use, and she often opened the dresser drawer and looked at the feed sacks and lace that her mom had put aside for her dress. She wished the material with the pretty flowered design could magically turn into a dress, but she knew that was impossible.

"Do you know how to sew?" she asked her dad, but he smiled sadly and shook his head.

The night before Easter, the father and daughter both went to bed with heavy hearts.

"I miss Momma," the little girl told her father.

"I know," he said. "I miss her, too."

"Jesus rose from the dead," the little girl said. "I wish Momma could, too."

"She will someday," he said. "That's what the Bible tells us."

"But not in time to make me a new dress for Easter?" the little girl asked.

"No," he replied. "I'm afraid not."

He kissed his little girl, tucked her in, and went to bed himself. They would have to get up early in the morning for the sunrise service, even if they didn't have new clothes to wear.

Both slept restlessly. During the night, the little girl dreamed she heard the sound of the sewing machine. She woke up and listened, and she could almost see her mother there in the other room. She went back to sleep and continued to dream.

It was still dark when her father woke her for breakfast.

"Look in your closet and find something to wear," he called to her.

She got out of bed and started to the closet, but something on her chair caught her eye. She moved closer and saw two things.

"Daddy! Daddy! Come quick!" she shouted.

He hurried in to see what she was excited about, and couldn't believe what he saw. There on the seat of the chair was a beautiful dress with a design of spring flowers and white lace stitched around the collar. Then his gaze went to the back of the chair. There hung a new shirt for him made out of white flour sacks.

They had certainly had no visitors in the night, so where could the clothes have come from? Did the mother return to make sure they would not have to wear old clothes? Had they had a visit from an Easter ghost? Would they ever know the answers? To them, it was a miracle they simply accepted.

The father and his daughter felt especially lucky that morning as they wore their new Easter clothes and attended the sunrise service, where they thanked and praised the Lord for everlasting life.

Easter Bunny

Roberta's Great-Grandmother Alley loved sentimental stories, and her daughter, Grandma Simpson, passed a few of her stories on.

Great-Grandmother Alley was staying with friends in northern Kentucky for a short visit at Easter. She had arrived a few days early, and she was enjoying helping out with the Easter preparations.

This was a time when families wore new clothes to the Easter church services, came home to a delicious meal, and then conducted an egg hunt for the children in the family. Tina, the family's young daughter, had received an Easter gift early, a rabbit that she named Bonnie Bunny, and she played outside all day with her.

The sun was going down when her mom called everybody in for supper. Tina put Bonnie down for a second while she got up from the ground, and that was all the time Bonnie needed to hop away.

Tina ran after her calling, "Bonnie, stop! Come back!" Bonnie had a head start and great running ability, so she disappeared into the woods by the road before Tina could possibly catch her.

Tina hardly touched her supper.

"Do you think she'll be okay?" asked Tina.

Tina's father thought of Mr. Tate's hunting dogs that ran loose beyond the woods. He didn't have much hope for Bonnie, but he smiled and said, "We'll have to wait and see. Let's say a prayer for her before we go to sleep."

Tina said her prayers and went to sleep. Her mom and Great-Great Grandmother Alley went to choir practice for the sunrise service at the church. All was quiet in the little town except for the occasional strains of music floating from the church.

Then, as they were walking home from choir practice, a neighbor, old Miss Bea Claiborne, vanished, and Bonnie Bunny came back in a dream. Great-Great Grandmother Alley and Tina's mother did not know about either occurrence until morning.

At an early breakfast on Easter morning, Tina's father related the disturbing news that Miss Bea had not made it home the night before.

"She walked out in front of us," Tina's mother said. "I can't imagine what could have happened."

Of course the sheriff and his men were out looking for the old lady, but there was no news yet.

"I talked to Bonnie in my dream last night," said Tina. "She said she couldn't live with me anymore."

"Why?" asked her mother.

"Because she's in heaven now. But she said she will come visit when I need her," said Tina.

The three adults at the table were trying to think of

something to say in response when Tina pointed at the window and exclaimed, "Look! There! She's here now!"

They all rushed outside, and watched Bonnie hop very close and then hop away. She kept up the routine. Back and forth!

"I think she wants us to follow her!" said Great-Grandmother Alley.

Bonnie hopped slowly enough for them to keep in sight of her. At a small drop-off in the road, she hopped down the bank. Tina, her mom and dad, and Great-Great-Grandmother Alley looked over. There lay Miss Bea Claiborne! She had twisted her ankle and had fallen down the bank.

Once they had taken care of rescuing Miss Bea, they went home and got ready to go to church. Tina dressed quickly and was outside with Bonnie when the others came out.

"It looks like Bonnie is back to stay," said her mother.

"No," said Tina. "We are saying good-bye. She came to help find Miss Bea. She has to go back now. I told you she's not real."

"Of course she is!" said Tina's mom.

She reached down to pick up Bonnie, but her hands went right through the little rabbit. It was Easter, and Bonnie Bunny had come and gone.

Easter Cross

Grandfather Simpson traveled all over Kentucky. He worked where he could find work, and then came home when he could. He was the grandfather Roberta never met, but everybody says he was the true storyteller in the family. He told Roberta's sister Fatima this story. He knew the people involved.

It was a beautiful, sunny Easter morning somewhere near Madisonville, Kentucky. After returning home from church, Steve and Grace Hawkins decided to take their three children on a picnic.

The park they chose had plenty of space for the children to play after they had eaten, but the play area was bordered in back by thick, dark woods.

The Hawkins twins, Ralph and Rachael, were almost nine, and the baby girl, Lana, was only four.

"Keep an eye on your sister," called Grace to the twins. "And don't any of you go into the woods."

The children had brought a ball, and they played happily in the open space in the park. Steve and Grace packed up the remains of the picnic and sat back to relax and enjoy the scenery.

"Didn't there used to be a cross over there by the road?" asked Steve.

"Yes," said Grace. "A child was killed there a few years ago and the family put up a cross at the site. The city made them take it down."

"Oh, yes," said Steve. "I remember that now. Officials said it was distracting because it was too tall or something."

Just then a car pulled in, and Steve and Grace were surprised to see her sister's family. Suddenly there were three more children to play with the Hawkins children. They were all delighted.

Time passed quickly as the two couples caught up on family news and local gossip. The children ran and squealed as they became involved in their ball game. Before they knew it, the sun was going down and it was time to leave.

"Come on, children," called Grace. "It's time to go home."

Grace's sister and her husband gathered up their three children, and Grace and Steve told Ralph and Rachael to get in the car.

"Where is your sister?" asked Steve.

"I don't know," said Ralph. "She was sitting in the grass by the woods watching us play the last time I saw her."

They all looked quickly around the park, but Lana was nowhere in sight.

"Lana!" Grace called, as she ran toward the woods. "Where are you?"

There was no answer. Grace realized that her little girl was gone.

Both families searched in the woods close to the park, but they saw no sign of Lana. They decided that they needed help because it was getting dark fast, so they called the sheriff.

Help came, but the hours were a blur for Steve and Grace Hawkins. At first, they scolded their children for not watching their sister, but they apologized after realizing they had really been the ones who had been neglectful.

"I'll never forgive myself if anything happens to her," said Steve.

"Me either," said Grace. "What was I thinking? She is only four years old!"

Darkness came, but the moon came out, giving a little more light for the searchers. The hours dragged on.

Finally, the searchers came to the front of the park to regroup and discuss what to do next. Everybody was focused on the park until they heard a faint voice.

"Mommy!" a child's voice said.

All turned to look toward the street where the voice came from.

There stood Lana, safe but exhausted.

Grace and Steve ran over, and Steve scooped her up in his arms.

"Lana, what happened?" Grace asked.

"I went after a bunny rabbit, but I got lost. I called, but you didn't hear me," Lana told her. "I just walked and walked, but I couldn't find my way back until I saw the cross."

"What cross?" asked Steve.

"The one by the road," said Lana.

"There hasn't been a cross there for a long time," said Steve.

"Look," she said, pointing to the place where the cross used to stand.

They all looked. With the moonlight shining on a large tree it did give the appearance of a cross! They stood looking, awestruck.

"I followed the cross and it brought me here," said Lana.

As they watched, the moon went behind a cloud and the image of the cross disappeared.

Thanks and good-byes followed, and then they all went home.

They wouldn't remember much about the food or the games, but no one there would ever forget the miracle of the cross.

Mother's Day

Tributes to mothers go back to the early Greeks, the Romans, and Christians who honored Mary, the mother of Christ.

In the United States, Mother's Day began around 150 years ago. Anna Jarvis, an Appalachian homemaker, organized a "Mother's Work Day" to raise awareness of poor health conditions where she lived. After she died in 1905, her daughter, also named Anna, campaigned to create a special day honoring mothers. In 1914 Anna's hard work was rewarded when Woodrow Wilson signed a bill recognizing Mother's Day as a national holiday.

Mother's Day is celebrated on the second Sunday in May. It has become the most popular day of the year to dine out, and also has the highest number of phone calls.

Anna Jarvis was angered by the increasing commercialism connected with a holiday she had meant to represent sentiment instead of greed and profit. It is said that before her death in 1948, she confessed that she was sorry for starting the Mother's Day tradition.

Despite her regret, however, the holiday is a wonderful time to honor and express appreciation for our mothers. As the stories in this section will show, mothers are with us always.

Mother's Day Tea Party

Roberta has a story about her Aunt Maggie and a special tea party her uncle told her about.

Little toy tea sets were popular when I was a girl. I had one that Aunt Maggie sent to me, but I had no idea of what a tea party was. I loved the beautiful designs in the cups and saucers, and I played with my tea set every day. Aunt Maggie had had tea parties when she was growing up in the city, so she thought that I would enjoy pretend tea parties, too.

I knew nothing about English tea, Japanese tea, or any tea drunk for pleasure. We used tea to cure all kinds of ailments, so to me tea was medicine. Mom said Grandma Simpson seemed to know about a bark, root, or herb that could be brewed to treat anything.

We drank coffee or milk with our meals, and we never drank anything but water between meals, so I pretended that my doll and I were eating regular meals when I played with my tea set.

After Aunt Maggie died, teatime became special for my uncle, as it had been for his wife. He always knew how much Aunt Maggie enjoyed her teatime.

Years earlier, Aunt Maggie was expecting a baby. She

hoped it would be a little girl. She saw a lovely tea set at the store and bought it and put it aside.

"What if it's a boy?" her husband asked.

"Then he'll have to learn to like tea parties," said Aunt Maggie.

Aunt Maggie looked forward to pretend parties with her child when it was old enough to play with the set. Sadly, that was not to be.

Aunt Maggie learned country ways when she married my uncle and moved from the city. She learned how to grow a garden and can food. She kept her canned fruit and vegetables on shelves in the basement, where they would be handy when she needed them.

A few days before her baby (which turned out to be a sweet baby girl they had decided they would call Jean) was due, Aunt Maggie went down to the basement to get a jar of green beans for supper.

As she turned to go back upstairs, she tripped on an empty box that had been left near the shelves when she had brought some canned fruit down earlier. She lost her balance and fell hard on the basement floor.

My uncle heard her scream and ran to the basement, where he found Aunt Maggie in great pain. He rushed her to the doctor, but she died in childbirth giving life to Jean.

It was hard raising a baby alone, so family members pitched in to help out. They were amazed at how fast Jean grew and learned. She would puzzle them sometimes by looking at someone they couldn't see and saying, "Mama."

Eventually my uncle remarried, and his new wife loved Jean as her own. One day she found the tea set in the closet and got it out to show Jean. Jean loved it right away. She was only four years old, but she played with the tea set every day.

That Mother's Day, Jean got out her tea set and carried it from her room to a small table by the basement door. She had never done that before. She always played with it in her room.

My uncle and his wife began to hear Jean talk. To their surprise, they heard a muffled voice answering the little girl! They couldn't hear what was being said, but they hurried to see who had come inside their house uninvited. There was nobody there but Jean, looking happily across the table.

"Is somebody here?" my uncle called out.

There was no answer.

"Jean, who were you talking to just now?" he asked.

"Mama," Jean answered. "She came to have tea with me because it's Mother's Day."

"Where did she come from?" his wife asked her.

Jean looked at them both very seriously and pointed down toward an area in the basement just beyond by the kitchen door.

"She came from down there," Jean told them. "That's where she stays so she can visit me."

My uncle turned pale. He had never told Jean or his second wife exactly where he had found Aunt Maggie that day. Yet Jean was pointing down, and he knew that under the kitchen floor in the basement was the exact spot where Aunt Maggie had taken the fall that resulted in her death.

Was Aunt Maggie the unseen presence through the years that Jean had addressed as "Mama?" Had Aunt Maggie picked Mother's Day as a special day to come back in spirit form to have a tea party with her daughter?

It was a lovely thought that maybe she did!

A Mother's Way

Mrs. Karnes was a neighbor who sometimes joined Lonnie's family in storytelling sessions when Lonnie was a boy. His family had moved from Adair County to Russell County because Lonnie's dad liked to build houses, sell them for a profit, and move on to another.

On Mother's Day everyone finished their chores early. Only necessary work was done on Sundays—gathering eggs, feeding the chickens, feeding and milking the cows, and feeding the mule and horse. Of course, meals had to be prepared and dishes washed, but that left plenty of time after supper for visiting and storytelling.

Most families finished their chores about the same time. It was getting dark when Mr. and Mrs. Karnes came to Lonnie's house that Sunday to sit and talk until bedtime. The conversation turned to mothers because it was Mother's Day, and the different ways people celebrated with their moms.

"My mother planted flowers at every place we lived," Lonnie's mother said. "There was nothing she liked better."

"My mom liked flowers, too," said Mrs. Karnes. "We made a point of taking a walk together on Mother's Day so she could pick the ones she especially liked. She would always gather a beautiful bouquet of wildflowers and bring them home.

"I never had her way with flowers," Mrs. Karnes continued. "We would walk the same path by the fencerow, across the field, down by the woods, and follow another fencerow back home. If she could see the flowers along the way, I should have been able to see them, too, but I'd walk right over them."

"Maybe I'll leave you my gift of spotting flowers when I die," Mother joked.

"I laughed," said Mrs. Karnes, "because I still had Mother around to find wildflowers for me. I didn't need to do it myself."

"I noticed that some beautiful ones have bloomed out," said Lonnie's mother.

"I noticed that today, too, for the first time!" said Mrs. Karnes. "After Mother died last winter, I still needed to take that Mother's Day walk today. I took the walk alone, and I had no luck at first finding the rare blooms. As I was walking along a fencerow on my way home, I suddenly felt a presence beside me. I felt like it was Mother. I looked around me and then I saw all kinds of pretty flowers in the field along the fence. I wanted to pick some, but I was so unnerved that I hurried along home without picking the flowers.

"When I got near the front porch, I noticed something by the steps. When I got close, I saw that it was a beautiful bouquet of fresh wildflowers!"

"I guess she did leave you her way with flowers," Lonnie's mother said to her.

"Yes," said Mrs. Karnes, "I think she did. And I think she left a last bouquet for me. My whole family was busy doing other things and had not been out of the house, so I know they did not put the flowers there. I can hardly wait to see if she comes again next year to take a walk with me."

Aunt Viney Rocks!

This is a Simpson family story that we never took too seriously, but we always enjoyed it because it was about Aunt Viney (Roberta's great-aunt), who was a stubborn, colorful character. She was not a mother herself, but her involvement in Roberta's family reflected her mother-like connection to everyone.

This is the story Roberta tells about her aunt.

Aunt Viney always came to visit at Grandmother Simpson's farm on Mother's Day and stayed for a week or two. She enjoyed the good food we always had for Mom and Grandma. It was a time when crops were planted, flowers were blooming, and the clocks were set forward one hour.

Back then where I grew up, time was either "fast time" (Eastern Standard Time) or "slow time" (Central Standard Time). Aunt Viney never cared for fast time, so her body operated on slow time. She didn't bother changing her clocks. She depended on her own body to tell her what time it was. It seemed to work well for her. She got up at the same time every morning and was usually ready for bed at the same time every night. Sometimes, she would look up at the sky;

I think she got some help from studying the position of the sun.

When she was visiting us, she liked to take early morning walks through the pasture looking for berries and wild greens. There she would inevitably encounter Uncle Josh's "butting ram." Everybody but Aunt Viney tried to avoid confronting that ram, but Aunt Viney let nothing get in the way of what she was pursuing. The ram would spot her and paw the ground. Aunt Viney would raise her cane and call out to him, "Butt me if you dare!" That animal never had the guts to take her on! Even this aggressive ram seemed to realize that Aunt Viney was one stubborn lady with an iron will, so he didn't waste his energy on a useless battle.

She would invariably return from her walk with greens or berries to cook for supper. She would sit in the old rocking chair and "look" her gatherings to see if there were any worms or insects in them. Then she would pass them to Mom or Grandma to cook later. As the sun moved high in the sky, Aunt Viney would begin to get sleepy. She would sit in the old rocking chair and would doze off for her afternoon nap. After supper, she would reserve that rocking chair, where she would rock and listen to music or stories provided by our family members. On Mother's Day, she always rocked while Mom and Grandma prepared the meal. Her contribution was to provide berries and greens. She was not too fond of cooking.

"Aunt Viney," my sister was once brave enough to ask, "why do you always sit in that rocking chair? What if someone else wants to sit in it?"

"It's comfortable," Aunt Viney replied. "If somebody else wants to sit in it, then it's their bad luck. I'd come back from the grave to sit in this chair."

She had a droll sense of humor, but it was lost on my sister. She never could figure out if Aunt Viney was joking or not, and she didn't pursue the conversation.

Aunt Viney went home soon after the holiday was over, but we knew she'd be back to visit the next year.

"Take care of my rocking chair," Aunt Viney always told my sister. "I'll be back in May to rock in it while the other women fix dinner."

The year passed. Then, a few days before the next Mother's Day, Aunt Viney died of a fever. It seemed strange to think that there should be anything, even a fever, that Aunt Viney couldn't conquer. Attending her funeral brought home the truth to my sister and me that she was really gone. We knew we would miss her annual visit.

Mother's Day came, and the house was filled with the smell of good food that morning. Everyone was looking forward to celebrating the day with the traditional meal.

There were no fresh berries or greens this time, because there was no Aunt Viney to pick them. My sister and I watched the rocking chair, but it did not move.

Other things proceeded as usual. The clocks had already been set ahead one hour. Mom and Grandma had spent the morning cooking. The table was set for the midday meal, and the family all wished Mom and Grandma a Happy Mother's Day.

"I wonder if Aunt Viney will come rock in her chair," my sister said. "She said she'd be back."

Everybody smiled and gathered around the table. As we ate, we glanced now and then at the rocking chair. It didn't move. After the meal was over and the table was cleared, everyone sat back in silence, letting the pleasant feeling of a good meal dominate the room. Obviously, Aunt Viney wasn't coming.

Then, suddenly, the silence was broken by a creaking sound. Everyone turned to look at the rocking chair, and much to our amazement, the chair had started rocking by itself! My sister was the first to speak.

"Aunt Viney's late!" she said. "She should have been here an hour ago!"

We glanced at the clock, but it was ticking away on time.

"No, she's on time," Grandma said, smiling. "You know how she hated fast time. By slow time, she made it right on schedule!"

We moved away before the next Mother's Day. We moved closer to town, and Uncle Josh was moving to a farm he had bought in Glasgow, Kentucky. Grandma was going to live with Uncle Josh. The old rocker was left behind.

We drove by the old place the summer after we had moved. The old chair was still there! We wondered how it would survive the winter. We wondered if the new owners of the old place would keep it and, if they did, whether Aunt Viney would come back to rock the next year. Would she wonder from the spirit world where the family had all gone?

Or would she have any sense of time passing from where she was on the other side? We never learned the answers to those questions, but we believe that wherever she is, Aunt Viney rocks!

Lena and the Lilacs

Lonnie tells a story from his boyhood about a woman who loved lilacs.

When I was young, Mom and Dad bought a house near the Miller Fields in Adair County. It hadn't been occupied for a year or two, but it was in good condition. A good cleaning and some paint were all it needed. My mom, Lena Brown, thought the yard also needed some flowers for color. The house demanded her attention first, though. It was early spring and she would have time later to plant some flowers.

She assigned easy chores for us children, while she and Dad tackled the more difficult things. Dad was busy with planting, while Mom cleaned the house and painted the walls. We helped by doing dishes after meals, washing windows, sweeping the floors, and cleaning up the yard.

Everyone noticed that the previous owners had dug up their favorite bushes and took them along to replant when they moved. The yard looked drab without anything growing. Mom was giving some thought to what she would like to plant. She was still undecided when something happened to influence her decision.

The first week we lived in the house, Mom began to smell the strong scent of lilacs in the kitchen. She mentioned it at supper, and we smelled it, too.

"Where's that coming from?" Dad wanted to know.

No one had the answer. There were no lilacs in the yard, and Mom and the girls didn't wear perfume.

"If there has to be a scent in the house," Mom said, "I am glad it's something nice like lilacs! I've always liked them. My mother always grew them in our yard."

The smell of lilacs continued.

Mother's Day was approaching and we were trying to think of something to get for Mom.

"How about getting her some lilac bushes to plant?" Dad suggested. "They could be a gift from all of you."

"Perfect!" we all agreed.

Dad volunteered to pick up the lilac bushes for us when he was in town, and we surprised Mom with them on Mother's Day morning. She was delighted!

"You couldn't have gotten me anything I would have liked better," she said.

We all went outside to watch and help with the planting. Mom planted them up next to the road where old bushes had been. Just as we finished, we saw a car coming down the road. It was unusual for cars to come down our road because our house was set back from the main highway, so we all were interested to see who it was.

The car drove slowly by, and then stopped, backed up, and stopped again. A young woman got out and walked, smiling, toward us. She introduced herself as someone who used to live in our house.

"My mother loved this house," she said. "We had to move away because my father got a good job elsewhere and couldn't afford to turn it town. My mother grew lilacs along the road. She dug them up and took them with us when we moved. She planted lilacs on Mother's Day last year. She always missed this place, though, and wished that she could come back for a visit."

"That would have been nice," Mom said.

"My mother died a few weeks ago," the young woman said. "I am down here visiting some relatives and I thought I'd drive by the old place one more time. When I saw you planting lilacs, I had to stop. Mother would have been so happy to know that lilacs are growing here again!"

"I think she knows," Mom told her. She told the visitor how we had smelled lilacs ever since we moved in, and how that had influenced our choice of what to plant.

The young lady was pleased to hear the story. She thanked us, said good-bye, and drove away.

We went back inside the house, and, to our amazement, the scent of lilacs had vanished! We never smelled lilacs in the house again, but we always enjoyed their scent along the road.

Mom always felt that the visitor's mother did come back to the house one last time. She made her presence known by the scent of lilacs and gave us the idea of planting them in our yard. Once she had done that, she was content to move on.

Memorial Day

Memorial Day typically marks the beginning of the summer season. A U.S. federal holiday for remembering the men and women who died in service to our country, it is celebrated on the last Monday of May. Originally called Decoration Day, the holiday was established after the Civil War to honor those who had died in that war, but by the twentieth century Memorial Day had become a celebration to honor all Americans who died in military service.

General John Logan officially proclaimed the day a holiday on May 5, 1868; it was first observed on May 30, 1868.

Celebration of the day usually took the form of a family reunion, especially for those who lived in the mountains or rural areas. Families came together to clear family graveyards and decorate the graves of loved ones with flowers. Very often people attend a religious service and enjoy a potluck meal of the traditional "dinner on the ground," eaten picnic style.

Nowadays, some use Memorial Day to honor all dead, not just soldiers who died.

Some of the best ghost stories are about battlefields and those who fought and died for us.

Remembering the Dead

A friend once read one of our books and said, "Goodness! There are so many dead people in it!"

Of course she was right. The books we write are about ghosts, and there can't be ghosts without dead people.

We don't mean to be morbid. We remember the dead with respect, and we try to determine how they connect with the living. It is comforting to us to find evidence that death is only a change to another form, and that we live forever.

Roberta's Grandma Simpson probably influenced her attitude about ghosts more than anybody. To Grandma Simpson, ghosts were a natural part of life. She acknowledged their presence, but went on about her daily routine unruffled if she encountered one.

Roberta remembers one story she heard about her grandmother and Memorial Day and tells it this way.

One Memorial Day, Grandma Simpson set out early to walk to church and put flowers on the graves of family and friends before too many people gathered in the graveyard. She had a basketful of flowers and little time to place them on the graves, because she was expecting company and had to get back home to cook dinner.

She left her children of various ages (my dad included) home alone, as most people did in those days. She knew they would be all right because the older ones were responsible for taking care of the younger ones.

She walked down the lane from her house, turned onto the one-lane dirt road at the cherry tree, and walked toward the two-lane road where the cemetery was located.

It was a warm May morning, and Grandma Simpson was enjoying the fresh air. At one point, the dirt road ran between two high banks. As she reached that point, the warm air suddenly turned cold. She saw someone approaching her. As he came nearer, she saw it was a soldier in a Yankee Civil War uniform.

She climbed the bank on her side of the road and watched as he walked by. He looked straight ahead and gave no indication that he was aware of her in any way. After he passed, she climbed down and looked to see where he had gone, but he had completely vanished from sight.

Grandma Simpson went on to the cemetery and put her flowers on the graves as she had planned. When she got home, she told what she had seen.

"Why didn't you follow him?" asked my dad. "How did you know he wasn't coming here?"

"He was a ghost soldier in a different time," she said. "He crossed over into our time somehow. I knew no ghost soldier had any business coming here. Besides, I had to get on with my errand and get home to cook dinner."

"What do you think his business was?" asked her son.

"I don't know," she said. "I guess maybe all this Decoration Day activity stirred him up."

That was her attitude. She moved on to other things, and so did the children. No paranormal experience was going to interfere with her daily plans.

One thing that her children could count on in her daily plans was having them make several trips each day to carry fresh water from a large, cold spring under the hill in back of the house. Grandma Simpson loved a fresh drink of water. The water bucket was left by the kitchen door with a dipper or a hollowed gourd in it so everybody could help themselves.

All the children got a spooky feeling when they went near that spring. It was out of sight of the house and was surrounded by many trees, making the whole area cool and dark. The spring was always covered by shadows.

Since Grandma Simpson had no refrigerator, the shadows made the spring a good place to keep butter and milk cool. Grandpa Simpson had made a little "box" springhouse to put the milk and butter in so animals could not get to them.

Trees and shadows are not good for the imagination of a little kid going alone to get a bucket of water. My father and his siblings all agreed that they felt like something was watching them when they would go there, so they would fill their buckets and hurry up the hill so fast that they would sometimes spill some of the water. They tried not to spill any, though, for of course that usually meant another trip to the spring.

One day Grandpa Simpson came to visit. He and Grandma were separated, but he came to see the children. They were sitting around, talking and catching up since his last visit. They happened to mention to him about the creepy feeling they had of being watched at the spring.

"Could be the ghost of a soldier who was killed there," he told them.

That caught their interest.

"A soldier was killed at our spring?" they asked. "How did it happen?"

"I was told that a handful of Yankees and Rebels came up on each other at the spring back during the Civil War," he said.

"You mean a battle was fought at our spring?" asked Dad.

"It was more of a skirmish," Grandpa Simpson explained. "One Yankee soldier was killed before the others rode away."

Dad remembered the Yankee soldier Grandma Simpson saw on the road and figured that was the explanation. The dead soldier must have been trying to get back to his comrades.

With a story to put to the spooky feeling, the children weren't so frightened after that, but they always felt a little sad.

Memorial Day Riders

Lonnie has a story about ghost riders in the Smith Woods.

The Smith Woods in Adair County was the most mysterious place I ever lived. When I moved there as a boy with my parents, much of the 1,200 acres of trees had already been reduced to make way for houses. There was, however, still enough left to contain all the mystery I could explore.

My mother made sure that my brothers and sisters and I didn't venture into the heart of the woods.

"There are all kinds of stories about this place," she warned us. "There are sights and sounds that cannot be explained. There's no telling what is back there, so you all must stay close to home."

This only made me want to go back into the woods more than ever, but Mom was usually on the lookout and put an end to my plans.

We picked up bits and pieces of tales about things that happened in the woods. We didn't have any way of proving if the information was true or not, but we did know truly that people were afraid of those woods because they had encountered things they could not explain.

On Memorial Day, we followed the local custom of getting dressed up and taking flowers to the graves of the soldiers who had died for our country. It was a day to socialize with the living and to remember the dead.

While my mom and dad were chatting with other people who had come to the graveyard at the edge of the woods for the same reason we had come, I struck up a conversation with an old man who was visiting one of the graves.

"Have you lived here all your life?" I asked him.

"Yes," he answered. "I was born and raised here and I guess I'll die here."

"Did anything scary ever happen to you in these woods?" I continued.

"Oh, yes, lots of things," he said.

"What was the scariest thing?" I wanted to know.

"I guess I'd have to say it was what happened on a Memorial Day when I was about your age," he said. "I had heard about a Civil War skirmish back in the woods, and lots of men were killed. The story was that the rebels were ambushed. Yankee soldiers came riding through the woods and attacked! They say that you can hear the footbeats of the horses to this very day.

"I was warned that I should stay away on Memorial Day night," the old man continued, "but I sneaked into the woods anyway. I guess I didn't really believe I'd see anything, but I waited a little while to see for certain. I really don't know how much time had passed, but I was beginning to wish I hadn't come so far.

"I decided to go on back home when it suddenly felt like everything around me changed. I was not alone. Men were sleeping a little beyond me on the ground. Then I heard the sound of hoofbeats thundering toward me! I heard yelling and shots fired, and after a moment of panic, I made myself turn and run for home without looking back."

"Did you ever go back again?" I asked.

"Not on your life!" he said, shaking his head. "To this day, I can feel those hoofbeats shaking the earth as they passed me by. They come riding through the woods every Memorial Day night, but I will never go back to see them. I wouldn't advise you to go either, Sonny! I honestly believe that I went back in time, and if I hadn't run away, I would have been shot or trampled to death."

The old man walked slowly away through the graveyard, shaking his head, and I went home with my family.

That night at supper, I told the story the old man had told me.

"You'd better not be thinking of going to those woods to see if it's true," my mom said.

"Yes, son," said my dad. "It looks like a cloud is coming up, so I want you children inside."

After we had gone to bed, I opened my window and sat listening to the far-off thunder. Then I heard another sound. It sounded exactly like riders deep in the woods.

The thunder got closer and drowned out the hoofbeats. The breeze coming through my window was warm, but I shivered. Were ghost riders riding deep within the Smith Woods? Or was it only the rumble of thunder I heard? I would never know, and to tell you the truth, I have to admit that I was glad deep down that my mom and dad wouldn't let me go out that night!

Lest We Forget

In keeping with those who now believe that Memorial Day is celebrated to remember all the dead, we will continue our custom of including in our book a story about a family member or friend who has died, but who means more to us than words can adequately express. John C. Ferguson is such a person. We feel very strongly that John sent a message from beyond to help Roberta when she needed it most.

We met John many years ago when we were working with the Corn Island Storytelling Festival in Louisville. John was an excellent writer and storyteller, and we did many programs and attended numerous workshops together. John had incredible people skills and always had an interesting or funny story to tell.

John was a graduate of the University of Kentucky, a farmer, and the owner of a trucking company. For many years he was known as the Truck Driving Storyteller. After twenty-five years of trucking, he began concentrating on hypnotherapy. He was also well versed in nutrition.

We always looked forward to John's phone calls. Whatever he had to share was always entertaining or helpful. He shared our interest in the paranormal and gave us some fascinating and useful information.

John and Roberta both suffered from sinus problems. When the subject came up in phone calls, he would tell Roberta about a food supplement that helped him tremendously. She wrote the name down, but then lost the note. She kept meaning to ask John to tell her the name again, but she always forgot.

I'll ask him next time I talk to him, Roberta thought.

As is so often the case, with her and with other people, Roberta thought she would have plenty of time later; but, as we all know, we should never put things off. On Tuesday,

August 7, 2012, the unthinkable happened. John passed away at his home in Sonora, Kentucky.

When the phone rang that night, John's number came up on our caller ID. It was a little later than he usually called, but Roberta reached for the phone happily, wondering what John had to say.

"Hello," said Roberta.

It was not John's voice that answered. It was his wife, Carol, calling to give us the heartbreaking news. The whole world went on hold for Roberta. She couldn't believe what Carol was saying!

Months passed. Carol, as well as John's children and grandchildren and all of his friends, missed him terribly. He had seemed indestructible to Roberta. She couldn't believe that she would never hear from him again.

In May 2013, following John's death, Roberta got an awful sinus infection. Nothing, not even antibiotics, would clear it up. From Memorial Day until July, she could not breathe through her nose. She had no idea what to do. The condition was driving her crazy! She had to hold a Kleenex in her hand all the time.

Why didn't I ask John about that supplement? she thought.

Then Roberta got another phone call from Carol. We love her and her family, but our calls to each other are infrequent; we usually stay in touch via Facebook. Of course, Roberta was happy to hear Carol's voice after so many months.

"Roberta," she said. "I read some from John's journals every night. Tonight I came across this entry about a food supplement John thought you should take. I had the strongest feeling that I should call and tell you!"

Roberta couldn't believe she now had this information. As soon as their call ended, she went to the computer and ordered a supply.

Roberta asked her doctor about the capsules, and he confirmed that there was nothing in them to hurt her. Almost immediately after starting to take the capsules, Roberta's sinus problem began to clear up. She continues to take the supplement, and her breathing problems are gone.

Thank you, Carol, for passing on the message from John. Thank you, John, for remembering us on the other side and sending Roberta the one thing she needed!

This experience reinforced our belief that life goes on, and that our loved ones are still there for us. We have no doubt that John sent us the information Roberta needed through Carol. We wouldn't be surprised if we hear from him again!

Father's Day

Since the role of fathers is as important as that of mothers, it seemed only right to establish a day to honor them, too. There are differences of opinion about the origin of Father's Day. Some say it started in West Virginia, others say Washington State, and still others believe it began in Chicago. In any case, the idea to set aside a special day for fathers started in the early years of the twentieth century.

The most popular origin story credits Sonora Smart Dodd of Spokane, Washington. During a church service in 1909, she thought of how her father, Civil War veteran Henry Jackson Smart, struggled to raise his children alone after his wife died. Dodd's memories led her to request a special day to honor her father.

President Woodrow Wilson approved a special Father's Day in 1916, but it was 1924 before it became an official event when President Calvin Coolidge signed a resolution. President Lyndon Johnson issued the first presidential proclamation regarding Father's Day in 1966.

Now we celebrate fathers every third Sunday of June.

And in our hearts, we know they are always with us, in this world and the next.

Dad's Message

A neighbor told us of her encounter with her father after he had died. She said it was more helpful than frightening.

Laurie's father had always handled all the family affairs. Her mother never worked outside the home and knew nothing of family business.

Laurie's father was Cherokee and proud of his heritage. He had family records that proved his background, but he always kept them in a special place.

From time to time as his children were growing up, he would take out the papers and tell them all the family stories he knew. He said certain funds were available from the government to help young Cherokees through college, if they could prove their ancestry.

He kept all the papers in a leather bag that he never left lying around. Nobody knew where he put the bag, though. He didn't even tell his wife.

When Laurie's dad died unexpectedly of a heart attack, the family was able to find the deed to the house and the insurance papers. Her father's special family history papers, however, were not with these other formal documents.

The insurance was enough only to pay off the house. For the first time, Laurie's mother had to look for work to support the family. The kids were old enough to pitch in, but they barely got by.

Laurie was the oldest, and when she graduated from high school, there was no money to pay for college. She was determined to go so she could get a good job and help her brothers through, but it was going to be a long, difficult process. Her school counselor asked her if she knew there were some federal funds available to help Native Americans with college expenses if they could prove their ancestry. She thought of her father's papers, but had no idea where he had put them. Nobody in the family knew either.

Laurie tossed and turned that night. She woke about 2:00 a.m., amazed to see her father standing at the foot of her bed. She blinked her eyes to make sure she wasn't dreaming.

"Dad," she whispered. Somehow, she knew he was trying to tell her where to find the papers.

He didn't answer, but motioned for her to follow him.

Laurie was too amazed to move. She held on to the bed covers and stared at him, and slowly he faded away.

She dismissed her experience as a dream—until the next night. Again, she woke at 2:00 a.m. She sat up in bed and watched in silence as her father materialized at the foot of the bed again. Once again, he motioned for her to follow him.

This time, she got out of bed and followed him. Together, they went down the hall to the kitchen. He pointed to a cabinet that stood against the wall. Then he vanished.

"We have already looked in the cabinet," she said aloud, and went back to bed.

Next morning, she told her mother about the dreams, but they agreed that nothing could be in the cabinet.

On the third night, Laurie again woke up in the presence of her father's ghost. He didn't look annoyed with her; he just had the patient look he always had when he was trying to teach her something.

Again he motioned and again she followed him to the cabinet in the kitchen. He disappeared as her mother came into the room.

"What are you doing up?" her mother asked. "Did you have that dream again?"

"I don't think it was a dream," said Laurie. "I think the papers are in that cabinet."

"You know we looked on every shelf and in every drawer," said her mother. "If it is here, your father needs to give us a clue."

Laurie and her mother couldn't believe what happened next. The bottom cabinet drawer flew out partway. They had looked in that drawer before, but now they pulled it all the way out. Upon careful examination, they discovered that the drawer had a false bottom in it, and there were the missing papers.

Laurie was able to apply for funds and received financial aid in completing her college education.

"And guess what day I finally found the papers?" asked Laurie when she told us the story.

Together we said, "Father's Day!"

Spirits of the Upper River Road

This story was given to us by a dear friend from Hitchens, Kentucky, who has granted us permission to pass it on to you. He has asked that we not use his full name.

On bright June days, people we know usually do not have ghosts on their minds. Our friend Matt told us of a haunting experience that happened to him when relatives were visiting for Father's Day. We think it is a wonderful example of how this world and the next exist side by side and that all living things, like trees, for example, are connected and can communicate with us if we will only listen. Read Matt's story and see what you think.

My first wife, Francesca, and I lived in New Albany, Indiana, on the downriver side of the Ohio falls. At the time, I was employed as a draftsman in a Louisville firm, while my spouse worked on earning a graduate degree at nearby Indiana University Southeast.

We were good friends with one of Fran's classmates, Cynthia, and her boyfriend, Tony, and often visited with them in their turn-of-the-century home in the Highlands area of Louisville. Cynthia and Tony announced to us one day that they'd recently rented a small cottage—the gatekeeper's house on the former estate of a Louisville industrialist. They invited us to drop by some weekend and walk the grounds of the estate, which bordered the left bank of the Ohio River and ran parallel to the very rural upper River Road section of the city.

We enjoyed a beautiful, late spring Saturday visiting with our friends, seeing the gatekeeper's house, and picnicking all by ourselves on the immense grounds of the old estate, which had actually served as a summer residence away from the city for the industrialist and his family. We noted that the mansion was gone. According to Tony, it had been severely damaged by fire in the late 1940s and was eventually torn down. What remained of the mansion complex was a large, mosaic-tiled swimming pool, as well as some of the pillar bases and floor tiles that still served to outline the original bathhouse. Cynthia mentioned that the current property owners were pleased to be able to rent the gatekeeper's house to her and Tony, as the owners needed the on-site security that renters would provide. Eventually the owners hoped to subdivide the former estate into building lots and develop the entire property as a high-end residential subdivision along the river.

It was hard for Fran and me to imagine such a lovely and pastoral landscape of woods and meadow being bulldozed and refashioned as make-believe country homes for the upwardly mobile. As Fran and I thanked our hosts and readied to depart for home, Cynthia told us to stop by anytime and walk the grounds, even if she and Tony weren't at home.

One month later, near Father's Day, Fran's parents came down from South Bend to visit us for a couple of days before heading on to the Maryland shore. On their last day with us, I suggested that we take them out to see the old estate on the river where our friends lived. Fran was rather hesitant at first to take her folks there; she was concerned that Tony and Cynthia might not be at home. I reminded Fran that our friends had extended an open invitation to us to visit the grounds anytime. The property was always open, and the owners had never posted "No Trespassing" signs on it. With some trepidation on Fran's part, we set out for River Road in Fran's father's new 1973 Cadillac.

It was a glorious June day, with weather like we enjoyed during our visit to the estate in the previous month—blue skies, wall-to-wall sunshine, and comfortable temperatures as Fran's father, Vince, drove the Caddy up the drive and to the turning circle, where we parked under a young elm. We got out and walked around the grounds—pretty much the same as where we'd walked earlier with Tony and Cynthia.

After we'd been there no more than twenty minutes or so, Fran pulled me aside and said, "I think we'd better leave."

Fran had always been in tune with the spirit world because she had lost both of her birth parents in her adolescence, but I didn't make the connection that something was wrong. I just assumed other persons, maybe the new owners, were on the property and headed our way.

Fran's parents came up to us and seemed to be ready to go as well. We all stood facing the old swimming pool and had our backs to Vince's Cadillac. Suddenly, there was a sharp "crack" sound from behind us. As we turned, a large limb from the elm tree came crashing down onto the hood of the car. The base of the limb had to have been at least six inches in diameter, but by some stroke of luck, just the younger, slimmer branches had come to rest on the vehicle's hood and windshield.

Without saying a word, all of us rushed to the car and began manhandling the tree limb off the hood. There was little damage—just some faint scratches on the hood and nothing more.

After we quickly pushed the limb to the side of the parking circle, Vince started the Cadillac. In seconds we were back on River Road and headed for the city and the bridge.

Once we felt we were out of harm's way, Fran's folks and I started talking about what had just happened. We all agreed that there had to be some logical explanation of what we had just experienced. Yet it was a cloudless day. There was no one else around the tree or even in close proximity to it. It was a green and seemingly healthy tree. The limb had not been cut.

While the rest of us tried to analyze the situation, Fran remained silent as the Cadillac sped back to our apartment. Months later, Fran confessed to me that she'd heard voices and laughter, and the sound of clinking drink glasses that ghostly day as we headed away from the pool toward the car.

Never before that day had I been convinced there was a spirit world.

When we heard Matt's story, we wondered whether the partiers had made the limb fall as a warning that trespassers were not wanted at that particular celebration long ago. It could have been a Father's Day get-together where only family was welcome. Maybe the ghostly revelers saw Matt, Fran, and her parents as party crashers. In any case, it is a fascinating tale of walking back in time.

Independence Day

Independence Day, July 4, is a federal holiday honoring our nation's birthday. It commemorates the signing of the Declaration of Independence on July 4, 1776, which marked our independence from the kingdom of Great Britain.

The first recorded use of the name "Independence Day" was in 1791. The U.S. Congress made Independence Day an unpaid holiday for federal employees. In 1938, Congress made Independence Day a paid federal holiday.

We celebrate July 4 in many ways—with picnics, concerts, parades, political gatherings, speeches, and fireworks! Macy's, in New York City, sponsors the largest fireworks display in the country.

Considering Americans' depth of feeling for freedom and our country, it is no wonder that spirits from the other side come back to this side to visit on the Fourth of July.

The Sinkhole

On February 12, 2014, we were shocked to hear that a massive sink-

hole had opened up under the Corvette Museum in Bowling Green, Kentucky, and swallowed up eight cars that the news described as "vintage and rare Corvettes." We are used to sinkholes in Kentucky, but they are usually small and do not do damage of this magnitude. We only knew of one large sinkhole that opened up on an uncle's farm in Glasgow while he was plowing, but even though it was deep enough to require help getting out, he and the tractor did not suffer too much harm. Still, it is a scary thought that the earth could suddenly open up without warning and gobble us up!

A sinkhole is an area of ground that has no natural external surface drainage, so the rocks beneath the land surface (like limestone and salt beds, for example) can be dissolved or eroded away. Geologists call this "karst terrain." Kentucky, Tennessee, Missouri, Florida, and other midwestern and western states are areas susceptible to sinkholes. Of course, we were not aware of all this technical information when we were growing up.

The news of the sinkhole in the Corvette Museum jogged our memory of a strange sinkhole happening that we could never explain. It happened to Roberta's cousin's family on Grandmother Simpson's old farm.

It started out like any summer.

Things slowed down after the end of school each year, and children enjoyed the lazy summer days that they could explore on their own at their own speed. Mother's Day and Father's Day brought special relatives to visit and special meals to eat.

Cousin Larry stayed to spend this particular summer

after the other relatives left. He had gotten in with the wrong crowd, and his widowed mother in Cincinnati thought he would benefit by spending time in the country, away from his new friends. We always liked Cousin Larry and welcomed his visits because we knew he would bring some excitement into our lives.

Larry always had new ideas to share with his country cousins. This one summer, which we would later call "The Summer of the Sinkhole," Larry decided that there should be a fireworks display on the farm on the Fourth of July like the ones he had seen in the city. He had some money with him that his mom had given him, but he needed to find a way to get more. Fireworks were legal back then and easy to come by, and there were several places to buy them in town.

As July approached, Larry and his cousin Earl sat in the backyard at night, trying to figure out how to earn enough money to buy the fireworks. They considered trying to get work helping on neighboring farms, but the crops were already planted and it was not yet time for harvest. Larry thought about sneaking out some of his uncle's watermelons and selling them, but there was no market for them because all the other farmers had planted watermelons, too.

While they discussed their plan for the fireworks, they enjoyed the warm summer breeze and the sight of the moon shining on the fields, the outbuildings, and the small sinkhole at the edge of the field where the backyard ended. Larry knew nothing about sinkholes, except that his aunt sometimes threw scraps and chicken bones in this one out back. Earl told him they must never play there because the sinkhole swallowed things up, but Larry thought little about it since it didn't have much appeal as a play area anyway.

The Fourth of July was getting closer and Larry still had no money for fireworks, so he was starting to feel a little desperate. Every day as he walked past the bedroom, he would notice a silver dollar and a few pennies in an old jar on the dresser by the door. Larry figured that the silver dollar, added to what he had, would give him sufficient funds to buy enough fireworks for a spectacular display. Nobody would miss it, he figured, and he could earn money in the city and send it back to his uncle at the end of the summer. So one day, when nobody was looking, Larry took the silver dollar out of the jar and slipped it in his pocket.

Larry couldn't wait to tell Earl that they could now proceed with their plans. They could walk to town in the morning and get the fireworks. After supper, he motioned for his cousin to follow him outside. He didn't stop near the house, but led Earl to the back of the yard and stopped beside the sinkhole.

"I've got the money," Larry whispered, even though there were just the two of them around to listen. "Look!"

He held the silver dollar in his hand in the moonlight. Earl recognized it immediately as one belonging to his father. It was a special keepsake that nobody was allowed to touch.

"Where did you get that silver dollar?" Earl asked.

"From the jar on the dresser in your dad's bedroom," Larry answered. "He'll never miss it. Besides, I am going to send him a dollar when I get back home."

"No, you don't understand!" Earl told him. "That's a special dollar. My grandpa gave Dad that silver dollar before he died. Dad keeps it for good luck. He wouldn't want to part with it. You've got to put it back!"

"Put what back?" asked a voice behind them. It was his aunt, coming to throw some table scraps into the sinkhole.

Startled, the two boys whirled around. The silver dollar flew from Larry's hand and landed in the sinkhole behind the scraps. Larry started to run into the sinkhole to look for it, but Earl stopped him. "What's going on?" Earl's mother asked the two boys. "What did you throw in that sinkhole just now?"

"It was an accident," said Larry. "I didn't mean to do it."

"It was Dad's silver dollar," Earl explained to his mother. He told her what had happened and that Larry was going to put it back. Earl's mother shook her head, very disappointed in the boys.

"It's too dark and dangerous to look in that sinkhole at night," she said, "but come on back to the house and tell your father."

That was what the two boys hated most to do, but they had no choice.

Larry's uncle was upset by what Larry had done, but after taking the lantern and going to the sinkhole to look, he agreed that it was not the time to look tonight. They would look for it in the morning. They went to bed, but Larry heard a thunderstorm during the night, and he feared it would not make the search any easier. He was right. The next morning, rainwater stood in the sinkhole.

Larry stood with his uncle and cousin by the sinkhole in the morning light. They could see no sign of the silver dollar.

"We'll have to wait until the water runs out and then look some more," said Larry's uncle.

Overcome by guilt, Larry ran down into the sinkhole toward the place he'd seen the scraps fall the night before.

"Come back!" yelled his uncle, but his order came too late. The sinkhole opened up like a big mouth in the earth and swallowed Larry down to his waist.

Earl ran to the shed where they kept some heavy rope, and together he and his dad pulled Larry out. Larry was scared and shivering, but unhurt. He told his uncle again and again that he was sorry; but even though his uncle forgave him, he worried about his lucky silver dollar the rest of the summer and often stood by the edges of the sinkhole to see if the dollar had surfaced. There was never a sign of it. The boys forgot all about the fireworks display that July.

When Larry left for home at the end of August, he said to his uncle, "I'll come back next summer and find that dollar for you."

The return visit was not to be, however. Larry's grades slipped during that school year, and his mother made him stay in the city and attend summer school. The family missed him on the farm, but they figured there would always be the next summer.

The family felt bad that Larry couldn't come this year, though, because the town council had decided for the first time to have a Fourth of July fireworks display near the little one-room school over on the main highway. The school was often used for community events.

Earl was excited because he would be able to see the fireworks from his backyard. The family moved their chairs outside when the fireworks started and watched the wonderful lights and patterns with wonder. They all agreed that Larry would have enjoyed watching them, too.

Suddenly a chilly wind blew on this hot summer night. Before their eyes, a shimmering light floated over the sinkhole. The fireworks wouldn't shoot this far from the school, but something was there for sure! For a moment, it looked like the form of a boy in the light, and then it vanished.

Amazing, they all thought, just staring at the sinkhole.

Together they moved to the edge of the sinkhole. Something shining in the moonlight caught their attention. Larry's uncle reached down and picked up the object. It was the silver dollar his father had given him. Larry was going to be so happy that it had turned up!

As they crossed the yard, they saw car lights coming.

"Now, who could that be at this time of night?" Earl's dad asked.

They walked toward the road and saw that it was the sheriff's car. The sight of it made them feel uneasy.

The sheriff parked by the road and walked up to them.

"Evening, folks," the sheriff said.

"Evening," they answered.

"I'm afraid I have some bad news, folks," he told them.

"Since you don't have a phone, I got the call at my office. I didn't want to wait to morning to let you know. It seems that your nephew Larry was riding his bicycle home from school this afternoon and a drunk driver hit him. He died in the hospital just a little while ago."

"Oh, no!" said Earl. "He was coming back next summer! He can't be dead! He just can't be!"

The family was numb with shock. How could that boy, so full of life and promise, be gone? Now he would never be able to come back and keep the promise that meant so much to him.

Or had he kept it after all? They thought of the shimmering light they'd just seen at the sinkhole. Had it been a trick of moonlight? Or was the shimmering light the ghost of Larry, coming back to shine on the lost coin?

Each summer after that, the family watched the local fireworks from their backyard and they always thought of Larry. Every one of them believed sincerely that Larry had come back that night and kept his promise. They hoped that wherever he was, he was enjoying the fireworks, too.

Blue Light Special—in the Graveyard and the Sky

Lonnie recalls another Fourth of July many years ago with his own cousins, when they also saw a strange light.

Back in the 1970s, my cousins were visiting from Ohio. One of my friends had joined us, and we were all sitting in the yard enjoying the July breeze. It was July 4, and we had already celebrated with fireworks and watermelon.

"Mrs. Brown," my friend asked my mother, "did you ever see a blue light in the graveyard?"

We could see the graveyard down the road from our house, and we all automatically turned and looked that way. At that very second, a blue light shot up from the graveyard into the air. We were all totally amazed at what we felt certain was just a strange coincidence.

"Well, I never saw one until now," said my mother. "Wonder what it is."

"I heard that it is an earthbound spirit looking for someone to take its place so it can go to heaven," my friend said.

"I never heard that," my mom told him. "But I don't have any other explanation," she admitted.

"Let's go down to the graveyard and see if we can find anything," suggested one of my cousins. "It might have been a firecracker."

"It didn't look like a firecracker to me," said my friend. "I think we should go and take a look."

All of us boys walked down to the graveyard and looked around with our flashlights. Nothing was out of place. We couldn't be sure where the light had been when we first saw it, but we headed to the back of the graveyard.

Then, suddenly, the blue light came back and danced on a grave in the back. That stopped us in our tracks.

"Come on," said my friend. "Let's get a closer look."

It took all of our courage, but we walked slowly toward the grave. When we got closer, we saw that the light wasn't on a grave at all, but on an empty plot next to it. The plot already had a tombstone, though; old man Reese had bought it for himself and had his name put on it.

As we reached the plot, the light lingered for just a moment before it vanished. In that time, we could tell that it wasn't a beam being projected from anything. It was a light unto itself, independent of any outside source. We had an eerie feeling, so we headed back home as fast as we could walk, trying not to look as frightened as we were.

The next morning, a neighbor came to tell us that old Mr. Reese had died last night on July 4, the night we saw the light. We thought all day about how weird was our experience of the night before.

That night, the same group was gathered in our yard. The sky was clear, and we could see the stars twinkling far, far away. We sat for a while, watching fireflies and listening to the pleasant night sounds. In the distance, a neighbor's dog barked now and then.

Suddenly, the fireflies disappeared and all the night sounds stopped. To any country person, that silence meant danger.

We looked around and up and saw a blue light streak from the graveyard into the sky.

"What's that?" I asked my father.

"I don't know," he said. "I've never seen anything like it before."

We sat, watching silently. The blue light seemed to be putting on a special show just for us.

It was obviously not an airplane. It could not have been searchlights or landing lights from an airport, because the nearest airports were in Lexington and Louisville. Its movements were too erratic for a plane, anyway.

It did not have a tail like a comet, nor did it fall like a meteor. Besides, it had gone up instead of down.

It stood still in the sky for a few seconds, and then it zigzagged back and forth and even moved in circles. It would go almost out of sight and then zoom toward earth in a flash. It seemed to be doing some kind of joyous dance in the sky.

The strange light continued this routine for about five minutes while we sat, transfixed. Then, finally, it swooped toward us once more, and then flew away toward the stars. We waited and watched for it to return, but this time it didn't come back. We had absolutely no idea of what we had been seeing.

"What did you say the blue light was supposed to be?" I asked my friend.

"It's supposed to be an earthbound spirit looking for someone to take its place so it can go to heaven," he explained again.

"Do you think it was an earthbound spirit that we just saw released?" asked my cousin. "Could Mr. Reese's death have released it?"

We were all wondering the same thing, but we didn't want to be the first to say it out loud. I was grateful to my cousin for speaking up.

We watched the graveyard every night when we sat out that summer, but we never saw a blue light again. None of us ever figured out what it really was. For us, that night of the blue light was very special.

Lake Stories

We grew up near Lake Cumberland, but it was not a major resort area then. It was just a quiet place along the banks of the Cumberland River where Lonnie and his father would fish.

Small family farms, which had been handed down from one generation to another, dotted the land along the shoreline. Most of the farmers had never lived anywhere else. They were not happy with the creation of the lake, but progress prevailed. In the end, they were relocated from their homes, and the farmland, homes, even whole towns and communities (such as Rowena, Horseshoe Bottom, Indian Creek, and others) were submerged in the lake. Eventually the pain the residents felt at losing what had been so important in their lives was mostly forgotten.

In addition to the submerging of the land, 123 cemeteries were relocated in the creation of Lake Cumberland. We recently visited one of the cemeteries where the dead were relocated. It is surrounded by woods, and the roads leading to it are narrow and tree lined. A hundred-year-old cedar tree stands in the middle of the graveyard. There is an eerie stillness about the site.

Were the dead disturbed by the move? Was the unhappiness of the displaced persons a negative force that remained in the lake?

Both of our fathers helped build Wolf Creek Dam, which was completed in 1952. They both expressed their concern many times about the future safety of the dam. It was built on limestone and a boiling spring, which made our fathers worry that there would be leakage eventually.

Sure enough, leakage started in 2007, and repairs on the dam were completed in 2013. During the period when the water level was lowered for safety reasons, local businesses and tourism suffered a big financial loss.

After Wolf Creek Dam was completed in 1952, the whole area changed. Now when we go back, we feel like we are in a different place from where we grew up. Recreation around Lake Cumberland is a big business now. There are boats of all sizes to rent, plenty of fish to catch, new places to stay and to eat, trails to hike, beaches to sun on, and many kinds of businesses where tourists may shop. The area is full of fun and entertainment.

We hear there are many strange things in Lake Cumberland. There are stories about catfish in the lake that are big enough to swallow a man!

A little girl once drowned accidentally in the lake. Two divers were brought in to find her. They surfaced saying there were so many dangerous things down in the lake that swimmers need to watch out.

The lake has its share of ghost stories, too.

Lady in the Lake

A legend that has persisted tells the sad story of a young girl who was very much in love. Unfortunately, the young man she loved did not love her. He led her on for a while, letting her believe that they would marry.

Finally, while they were both attending a Fourth of July picnic, she pressured her beloved to name a date. Fed up with her persistence, the young man told her that it was over. He said he did not love her at all; he had only been using her.

When the young woman realized that it was hopeless, she climbed to the top of one of the high cliffs along the shoreline and threw herself into the lake.

Since her drowning, it is said that if you swim in the lake near that cliff, she will swim to you and pull you under the water.

Maybe she is hoping that the man who broke her heart will come swimming by one day and she can have her revenge.

Summer Playmate

When we are telling stories or doing workshops, children sometimes ask if ghosts can be dangerous. Their questions remind us of a story that happened to a family we met on a Fourth of July picnic on Lake Cumberland.

Friends of ours had rented a cabin on the lake for an extended vacation. They invited us to spend the Fourth of July weekend with them. It was an offer too good to refuse.

The cabin's yard went up to a narrow beach beside the water. It was relaxing to sit on the cabin porch and look out over the lake, or to stroll along the beach and wade at the water's edge. We never went out more than a few steps. Signs warned of a drop-off near the shore where the water was deep for swimming.

Neither of us had any desire to swim in Lake Cumberland. We knew that when Wolf Creek Dam was built and the lake covered farms, houses, and landscapes, all kinds of things were left on the bottom. We had heard tales of huge fish, tangled barbed wire, and other spooky things that had at some point been harmful to swimmers. We were happy to stay safely on land. As we learned that weekend, that was a good decision.

A family named Jackson had rented the cabin next door, and they came over to visit late in the afternoon. Their little seven-year-old daughter, Tiffany, asked if she could walk on the beach.

Both parents said no in unison immediately.

"We had a terrifying experience here last summer," Mrs. Jackson explained. "We were staying in a different cabin than we have this year. It was about four cabins up the beach. Tiffany was allowed to play in the yard because it was fenced. We kept the gate locked so she would not be able to wander off.

"Tiffany began to come in each afternoon about sunset and tell us that there was a little girl alone in a boat on the lake.

"We couldn't imagine that anyone would allow a child to go out in a boat alone. When we would follow her out to see, the boat and the child were gone.

"Then Tiffany came in one day and said the boat was bobbing in the water and the little girl was walking on the beach, waving to her. 'She wants me to get in the boat with her,' Tiffany told us.

"That got our attention. We both told her that she must never, ever do that. We decided that night that we had better find where the girl lived and have a talk with her parents.

"The next day, after we finished supper we went out to watch the sunset. Tiffany had already gone out to play while we were cleaning up the kitchen. When we got outside, we were surprised to find the locked gate open. Then we looked at the lake and saw a boat with Tiffany in it, in the water right off the beach. The boat was slowly sinking, and Tiffany was screaming for us to come get her.

"My husband raced out the gate, across the beach, and splashed into the water. He pulled Tiffany out of the boat and carried her the short distance home.

"'What on earth were you doing in that boat alone?' he said to Tiffany. 'You know better than that! Couldn't you see the boat had a leaky bottom?'

"'And how did you get through that locked gate?' I added.

"'The little girl opened the gate and helped me in the boat,' Tiffany explained. 'She said it would be fun, but it wasn't.'

"The next day my husband went looking for the little girl and her parents. Nobody knew a family with a little girl. Then a man at the bait shop remembered something interesting.

"'There was a family with an eight-year-old girl that rented that cabin you're in a couple of years ago. The little girl sneaked out one night and took their old boat out. It was a windy night and the boat capsized and she drowned. We never heard anything about them after they left.'

"We still had a week of vacation left," continued Mrs. Jackson, "so we decided to keep a close eye on Tiffany. We made certain that the gate and the doors to our cabin were all locked.

"The first night, we thought we heard a voice, but decided it was only the wind. We were going back to sleep when we heard Tiffany call.

"'She's back!' screamed Tiffany. 'She wants me to go with her again. She says she wants someone to play with.'

"We ran to her room, and there was Tiffany, standing by the window, looking into the yard.

"We ran to her and looked in the direction she was looking. The moonlight was bright, and we could see clearly. The gate that we had locked a little while before was now open and swinging in the wind.

"We took Tiffany to our room for the rest of the night. The next morning, we packed, cut our vacation short, and headed for home.

"This year we rented a different cabin. So far we haven't seen anything unusual, but it doesn't pay to take any chances."

The Fireworks Night

July 4 brought great excitement to children in the country. This story about a tragic celebration comes from Wayne County and was told to us by Roberta's Uncle Lawrence and Aunt Lily Simpson.

Uncle Lawrence and Aunt Lily lived on a farm next to little Janis Miller. She was six years old and eager to see the fireworks display on the Fourth of July. Her father had bought plenty of fireworks and had invited all the neighbors to come watch when he set them off in the field behind his barn that night.

As the daylight began to fade, the neighbors arrived with chairs and blankets and picked a good spot for viewing the fireworks show.

Mrs. Miller had made lemonade for everybody, and they were all sipping their drinks and visiting with each other.

Janis ran around talking to everybody. She was dressed in a white blouse and blue skirt, and wore a red ribbon in her hair. She felt very patriotic that night.

"I wish it would hurry and get dark," she said. "I can't wait to see Daddy shoot off the fireworks."

Finally, she got her wish. It was dark enough to begin.

"Now, Janis, I know you're excited," her father said, "but I want you to promise me that you'll stay here with your mother."

"But I want to help you, Daddy," Janis said.

"Honey, fireworks are very dangerous. Sometimes they don't do what you think they are going to do," her father explained.

Janis was not happy to have to stay on the sidelines, but when the fireworks started, she got so involved that she forgot everything that had happened before.

The Millers' display was indeed spectacular. Janis loved the noise and the beautiful colors that filled the sky.

Then, one firework did not go up. It flew to the side toward the spectators and fizzled on the ground.

Without thinking of any danger, Janis ran and picked it up. At that second, it exploded in her hand.

Janis screamed and screamed before she died, and nobody could do a thing to help her. Her father ran and picked her up, and her mother fainted when she saw her face, or what was left of it.

Few people ever talked about what she looked like because it was too gruesome. Everybody tried to put that awful night out of their minds.

They say that most people don't want to go outside on July 4 near the place it happened. An explosion will fill the air, and the ghost of Janis Miller screams and screams in the moonlight.

July's Stormy Fireworks

Roberta had a strange experience one Fourth of July years ago. She tells the story this way.

Even though I am called the Queen of the Cold-Blooded Tales, I am deathly afraid of lightning. My family learned early on to stay out of my way if we were outside when a thunderstorm was approaching. If they didn't, they risked being trampled by my flying feet. I would feel sorry later, but at the moment I was seeking shelter, I cared about nothing in my way. I remember clearly when I decided that I had to do something about my problem.

We were at a neighbor's Fourth of July picnic when a little cloud passed overhead. Without any warning, there was a streak of lightning and a crash of thunder. I remember running across their yard, across the street, down our driveway, and into our house, but I don't remember passing anything or anyone until I got inside our dining room. I looked out the window and saw one of the guests that I had run by—and he was in a wheelchair!

Fortunately, he was a very self-sufficient man, and there were lots of people around to give him assistance if he had needed it, but that didn't excuse my blind panic. Of course, I had hoped that nobody had noticed my dramatic exit from the picnic, but it had been impossible to miss. My wheelchair friend teased me for a long time after that.

He would say, "I may need some help, Roberta. I think a storm's coming."

I knew I had to find some way to act in a rational manner in storms. I had to, because I had to be able to function in daily life regardless of the weather. I began to read everything I could find about lightning. I thought about my family background to find a reason for my irrational fear. I came up with some interesting information.

I knew that part of the problem was that lightning had

often shocked me when I was caught in storms walking home from school as a girl. Barbed-wire fences ran along the dirt road where I had to walk, and lightning would strike, run along those fences, and shock me. I can still feel that tingling sensation!

I also knew that my fear had increased when we got electricity in the house when I was about nine years old. Maybe things weren't grounded properly then, but lightning would strike, run into our house, burst lightbulbs, and shock me. I was even shocked once in a car when we stopped to let a friend out at his house. I realized then that lightning could get me anywhere.

I was sure, too, that my mother passed on some of her fear of storms to me. She was afraid of them because she had survived a tornado when she was a girl. Eventually she persuaded my father to build a storm cellar under our back porch. It offered protection in the storms and was also a good storage area for potatoes and canned goods. When storms approached, neighbors would sometimes join us in the cellar for shelter, but I was always the first one inside it.

I never met my mother's mother, Grandma Fanny Gentry Dean, because she had died when my mother was only nine years old; but I had heard about her fear of storms through my mother. One of Grandma Fanny's stories helped me finally deal with my fear.

Grandma Fanny had always been afraid of storms. When my grandfather was away from their little Adair County farm,

Grandma would watch the weather carefully. If a cloud came up, she would hurry off to stay with her neighbor, Mrs. Withers, because she thought Mrs. Withers's large house would be safer than her own.

One Fourth of July, Grandpa Mike Dean had some business in Russell County that would take all day, so Grandma Fanny stayed home alone. She had plenty of chores to do before he got back home that night. No fireworks or celebrations were planned for that night, but Grandma Fanny ended up with her own fireworks.

At noon, Grandma Fanny heated up some leftover pinto bean soup and cornbread, and just as she finished eating she heard thunder announce the coming of a very black cloud. Grandma Fanny closed the doors and windows and hurried up the road to stay with Mrs. Withers until the storm passed. The lightning was striking in the distance, and the whipping wind had already reached the road where Grandma Fanny was hurrying along.

She arrived with little time to spare before the storm broke. Grandma Fanny knew it was not safe to sit by doors, windows, or fireplaces when the lightning was bad, so she chose a chair in the corner by a china cabinet.

"That's a good choice," said Mrs. Withers. "Lightning struck the house once and shocked my mother who was sitting in that very chair!"

"Oh, my!" said Grandma Fanny. "Maybe I should sit somewhere else."

"No," said Mrs. Withers. "I was just going to say that she

didn't die from the lightning, but she was scared of lightning ever since. She said that lightning never strikes twice in the same place, so she would sit in that chair after that when she was here because she thought she'd be safe. She died of natural causes, not lightning, but I always think of her when it storms."

Grandma Fanny knew that what Mrs. Withers's mother believed was not true. Even though Grandma Fanny did not know some of the things we know today—such as the fact that the Empire State Building in New York is struck by lightning two dozen times or more each year, or that the shuttle launch pad at Cape Canaveral in Florida is struck over and over, sometimes more than once in the same storm—she knew of a neighbor man who had been struck by lightning five times. Lightning doesn't have a memory, so it does, can, and will strike the same place or object more than once.

That knowledge, of course, did not comfort Grandma. She became more and more fearful that she had picked the wrong place to sit. Mrs. Withers seemed to think it was the safest place, though, so she remained in the chair.

Grandma Fanny was sitting very still and growing more and more uneasy with each lightning strike outside, when suddenly she felt a push and she fell forward out of her chair. Mrs. Withers ran over and helped her across the room to the sofa. At that moment, lightning struck the side of the house just where Grandma had been sitting. The force of the strike knocked over the china cabinet, and glass shattered and flew into the now empty chair. Grandma would not only have suffered from the lightning strike, she would also have been cut by the flying glass if it hadn't been for that strange push.

Grandma told Mrs. Withers, "Something pushed me out of the chair! Maybe it was your mother."

"Oh, yes, it was Momma," replied Mrs. Withers. "She came back from the dead to save you from the lightning!"

"Maybe she did," agreed Grandma.

Grandma Fanny waited until the storm was over. Then she said, "I think I'll go on home now. I've still got chores to do, and I've had enough fireworks for one day!"

After that experience, Grandma Fanny decided that she was as safe at her house as she would be anywhere else. She didn't know if Mrs. Withers's mother had come from the grave to push her to safety or not. She didn't know if she had a guardian angel watching over her or not. She did know that some power beyond herself had saved her from injury or death in that storm, and she figured that power would be with her regardless of where she was in a storm. She never forgot that July 4 and passed the story on to her children.

I learned a lot from Grandma Fanny's story.

"Don't run from a storm," she would say after that. "Take the best precautions you can and leave the rest up to the Lord."

I am still afraid of lightning, but if I am caught in a storm while driving, I can maintain control of myself and stay rational. I hurry to shelter if I am outside, but I haven't run by any other friends in wheelchairs.

Oh, I still come inside and stay away from windows, doors, chimneys, and electrical sockets when it is storming. I unplug the television set and my computer. I don't cook when lightning is striking. I never take a bath, wash dishes, carry an umbrella, eat with silverware, wear jewelry, or talk on the phone during a thunderstorm. I always remember (and I advise you to remember, too) that if you can see lightning, it is capable of striking you. You might want to reconsider if you like to stand on the porch or in front of an open garage door and watch a storm approach. A friend of ours dashed to the yard in a storm to bring in items from his yard sale, when lightning struck and put him in a wheelchair for the rest of his life. It can happen.

I like to think we all have guardian angels like Grandma Fanny did that day. I don't want to try their patience, though. When it storms, you will find me inside somewhere doing what I can to protect myself before I call on those angels for help.

A July Day Revisited

Uncle Buck Rooks worked all day in the fields and was ready for a quiet Fourth of July night at home.

Uncle Buck was really Lonnie's grandfather, James Milton Rooks, but everyone called him Uncle Buck. Lonnie's mother, Lena Rooks Brown, told him many stories about Uncle Buck. He often encountered things that were most unusual.

On this July day, his wife, Zona Mae, met him at the door as he came in.

"Buck," she said, "we are out of lamp oil and sugar. Could you ride to the store and get me some?"

That meant a trip through the Smith Woods in the late, late afternoon to get to the store, and Uncle Buck wasn't eager to go. All kinds of tales were told about those woods. He wasn't a coward by any means, but it wasn't a place to be caught at night. Besides, he was tired.

"Can't it wait until morning?" he asked.

"Not unless you want to sit in the dark tonight," Zona Mae told him.

Uncle Buck knew he had no choice. He had to go. He saddled his horse and started into the woods. He had never taken the shortcut through the Smith Woods, but he had heard it led past the old Creech farm and came out right at the front of the store. Mr. Creech had died the year before.

As Buck told the story, he figured he was about halfway to the store when he came upon a field carved out of the thick timber. At the back of the field was a small cabin. He didn't think anyone lived there, so he was surprised to see an old man plowing in the field near the woods.

"Hello!" Uncle Buck yelled, but the old man didn't look up.

Uncle Buck rode on without attempting to get the man's attention again. It wasn't a good time to start a conversation anyway, since he was in a hurry.

The shortcut took Uncle Buck right to the country store.

He was glad he had come this way, because he knew that returning the same way would allow him to get back home before dark.

He talked for a few minutes with the store owner and bought his oil and sugar. As he turned to go, he thought of the old man he'd seen plowing. He turned back again.

"Has anyone moved to the farm back there in the shortcut?" he asked. "I thought nobody lived there."

"No," said the store owner. "Old man Creech used to live there, but he died last July 4. They said he worked in his field all day and then went in and died quietly. His heart gave out on him, I heard. Why? Why do you ask?"

"I took the shortcut here today and passed the little farm. It just got me to wondering, that's all."

Uncle Buck thought it best not to say he'd seen an old man plowing the field. He thought he'd look for the old man on his way home. He knew what he'd seen! He wasn't crazy. He would get the old man's attention this time and find out who he was.

When Uncle Buck reached the field, it was empty. There was no sign that anybody had been plowing. The little cabin looked as empty as the field.

Uncle Buck never bothered to try to find an explanation. It was obvious that no living person was there in that field. Maybe the ghost of the old man only wanted a quiet July night like Uncle Buck did. Maybe he had come back to revisit his last day on earth. If so, it wouldn't be right to intrude. Besides, Uncle Buck believed it was bad luck to disturb the dead.

Black Dog at the Foot Log

Roberta tells this story about her sister on a memorable Fourth of July when they were young.

We Simpsons had black dog stories and legends in our Irish history. I liked to hear black dog ghost stories when I was a small girl, because a black dog ghost comes to save someone in danger, not to frighten anyone. It was a comfort to me to think there was a ghost dog out there looking out for me in case I needed help.

According to legend, a black ghost dog appears between the person in danger and the danger itself. One must never pass a black ghost dog because the danger beyond the dog is usually deadly.

One night, my sister Fatima and my cousin Len encountered a black ghost dog that saved their lives.

Some of our city cousins often came to visit every summer where we lived on Grandma Simpson's farm. It was always a treat for my older sister, Fatima, and me to have their company. My sister was always especially happy when one of the male cousins came, because he was her age and could escort her to social events at neighboring churches to which she would never be allowed to go alone at night.

Cousin Len was visiting for the month of July, and he and Fatima learned that there was going to be a pie supper followed by a fireworks display for the Fourth of July at the church near Sano, Kentucky. They persuaded Mom and Dad to let them go enjoy the festivities. Fatima baked a chocolate pie and decorated a fancy box to attract bidding at the pie supper. Funds from the event were used to help with church expenses.

Few people had cars, and we were one of the families who didn't. Most people walked everywhere anyway. It wasn't too far to the church, and Fatima was very familiar with the way to go. You first walked down a one-lane road past the neighboring farm, across a field, and down a little slope to Russell Creek. Then you had to walk across a foot log to get across the creek. After that, you would go up a hill and right down the road to the church.

Foot logs were trees that had fallen across the creek or logs that had been placed across the creek to serve as a bridge. Sometimes stakes were driven in the ground on each bank, and a rope or chain was strung across the stream by the log to hold on to for balance. The log was just wide enough for one foot at a time, so the pedestrian had to be sure-footed and careful. The foot log was low over the water, so the worst that ever happened was that someone would occasionally fall off the log and splash into the water.

Len and Fatima crossed the creek on the foot log without incident. They went on to the church to enjoy their evening, with no thought of any trouble ahead.

Mother Nature sometimes has some bad trouble in store, though, and it can come without warning. There were no weather forecasts back then. We had a battery radio that we used sparingly so we would save the battery, but we had no television sets or computers. Telephones were rare, and the only one in our neighborhood was over a mile away at a general store. In short, communications were limited, and weather forecasts were not in our daily routine. Severe storms could be on the way without our knowing about them.

It was understood among families that if bad storms struck at an event close by, young people would stay at a house close to the event, even if it meant staying overnight. All the neighbors knew each other, so the visitors would not be spending the night with strangers. If the storms were over early enough, the young people went on home; but if the storms lingered, the young people stayed all night and went home the next morning. This Fourth of July night turned out to be such a night for Fatima and Len.

There had been no clouds in sight when they left home, but they heard distant thunder by the time they got to the church. While the pies were sold, the storm got closer. Everybody decided it was wise to stay inside and eat the pies, and it turned out to be a good decision.

When the storm hit full force, it was so strong that it seemed to be trying to blow down the walls and join the pie eaters. It was soon evident that the church's fireworks display would not be held that night, because Mother Nature had her own fireworks on display. Lightning lit up the sky with one flash after another, the wind howled, and the thunder boomed louder than any fireworks could do.

After those gathered finished the pies, they expected the storm to let up. Unfortunately, it didn't. It was getting to be bedtime, so most people decided to make a dash for home. A few had cars, and many lived near the church, but Fatima and Len had a long walk home. Everybody got drenched as soon as they stepped outside, so Fatima especially dreaded the long walk in the rain.

The Bryants lived next door to the church. They all ran for their house, but Mr. Bryant stopped on the porch and called to Len and Fatima.

"Why don't you come in and spend the night?" he asked them. "Your folks won't expect you to walk home in a storm like this. The creek is probably up by now anyway."

Fatima stopped, ready to accept his invitation, but Len called back, "No, I think we'll go on. I'm afraid Aunt Lillian will be mad at me if I don't get Fatima home."

"Well, come on back if you need to," he called. "We will be up for a while until the storm lets up."

"Okay, thanks!" called Fatima.

"All right, then," Mr. Bryant said.

The water was dripping off their faces and clothes as Len and Fatima headed down the hill to the creek. They were surprised when they got to the foot log. The creek had risen to the banks, with the water touching the bottom of the log. Looking at the rushing water made Fatima dizzy.

"I can't walk across that log," she told Len. "It's much too dangerous."

"Yes, you can," Len said. "Come on! I'll hold on to you."

"I can't!" she insisted. "Give me a minute."

Before they could move, they saw that something had

joined them. A black dog was standing between them and the foot log! When Len started to take a step forward, it let out a low growl, but didn't move.

"What's this?" asked Len.

"It's a black dog!" Fatima said.

"I can see it's a black dog!" said Len. "Where did it come from? Whose dog is it anyway?"

"It's a ghost dog," Fatima told him. "Haven't you heard of them? These dogs come to our family when there is great danger. If we walk by it, we'll die."

"I never heard of such a thing," said Len.

"I guess that's because they are on Dad's side of the family, and you come from Mom's side," said Fatima.

"That's crazy," Len said. "Come on!"

The dog didn't move and neither did Fatima.

"I'm not budging," Fatima told him.

Len stood there, trying to figure out what to do. Then, from out of nowhere, a wall of water came rushing down the creek and swept the foot log away from the banks and out of sight.

Len was amazed. He just stood there, frozen in his tracks.

Without a sound, the black dog vanished. It had accomplished its mission, and it wasn't needed anymore.

Len still stood staring at the rushing water.

He and Fatima both knew that they had just most likely escaped death. If they had passed the dog and walked out onto the log, they would have been swept away, too, and most likely drowned.

Fatima and Len had no choice but to return to the Bryants' house and tell them what happened. Mrs. Bryant gave them hot soup and dry clothes, and they finally got to sleep in spite of the storm that rumbled overhead all night.

The next morning, Mr. Bryant escorted Fatima and Len home. The creek had gone down; it looked as though nothing had happened. We were all glad to see them and excited to hear their story. The black dog had saved their lives, and their story lives on, too.

A Mystery at Cave Hill

Roberta has a story of one Fourth of July that she spent at a cemetery.

It was the Fourth of July, and Lonnie had to work that day. A friend came by with his two young daughters and asked if I would like to go with them for a walk through Cave Hill Cemetery. The daughters and I had never been there, so I eagerly accepted the invitation. I had heard that people had experienced spooky sightings there, but that was not uppermost in my mind that day. Cave Hill is more like a park than a cemetery. It was just a great day for walking, feeding the ducks, and enjoying the sunshine and fresh air.

We entered the cemetery and saw right away that it was beautifully kept. We noticed, too, that there were tombstones, statues, and memorials of all shapes and sizes. The cemetery was a natural setting for the dead, filled with trees, flowers, and blooming bushes.

We strolled around, visiting graves of famous local people, including Colonel Harland Sanders, Kentucky Giant Jim Porter, the Brennan family, and many more.

As we walked, we discussed some of the stories we had heard about people seeing glowing tombstones, strange lights, ghostly figures, and other mysterious things.

"Is this cemetery haunted?" one of the girls asked.

"Ghost hunters who have come here to do investigations report that there is spirit activity," I told them. "This is my first time here, so I haven't experienced anything myself."

We came upon a workman who was working on the grounds, so we stopped to chat.

"Are there ghosts here?" the other girl asked.

The worker smiled and said, "I haven't seen anything myself, but I have heard a lot about faces at the tombs, orbs, and all sorts of things like that. So I can't speak from personal experience, but this place is included on many lists of haunted places."

We moved on, allowing the man to get back to his work.

We then came upon the duck pond, which is a very popular spot in Cave Hill Cemetery. Much of the duck population is made up of pet ducks that grew to be too big for a regular yard. The idea was to release the ducks in a place where it would be possible for children to come and visit their grown-up pets.

The girls knew about the ducks, so they had brought bread to feed them. They shared some of it with their father and me, so we could feed the ducks, too. The ducks were happy to see us bringing food, so they rushed up to be sure they got something to eat. We soon exhausted our bread supply and had to say good-bye to the ducks and continue our walk.

I don't remember how long or how far we walked. We were mostly silent, just enjoying the sunshine and the peaceful surroundings.

Suddenly, the girls stopped and said together, "Look!"

We looked in the direction they were pointing. It was a tomb at the top of a small hill. We had to blink to make sure our eyes were not deceiving us, because in front of the tomb stood a misty, ghost-like figure. It seemed to be looking at us, too.

My friend and I started walking toward it, but when we had taken a few steps, the figure vanished. We were going to continue to the tomb to investigate, but the girls called out that they wanted to go home. Seeing that they were really upset, we turned, walked back to the car, and left.

I visited the cemetery another time, but I couldn't find the tomb and I didn't see anything spooky. I think that figure appeared on that first visit to answer our question "Is Cave Hill Cemetery really haunted?"

Labor Day

Other countries have holidays that honor workers, but we will limit ourselves here to stories related to the Labor Day holiday that is celebrated in the United States.

Labor Day was established as an official U.S. holiday in 1887 and is celebrated on the first Monday in September. Whether we think of it as the end of the summer or the start of a new school year, Labor Day is in fact meant to honor our nation's working people.

The pattern for Labor Day celebrations was outlined in the first proposal for the holiday. It recommended that there be a street parade to demonstrate the strength and spirit of trade and labor organizations followed by a festival for workers and their families.

We hope you will enjoy the following ghosts connected with this proud American holiday.

Labor of Love

No matter the season, there was always work to do on the farm. The fields needed to be plowed for regular crop planting, and fall plowing helped improve moisture and nutrient accumulation in the soil in a form accessible for plants. Some farmers planted cover crops such as turnips. Turning the soil over buried the sod, fertilizers, weed seeds, and many agricultural pests that were agents of disease. The lower side of the soil brought to the surface by plowing brought aeration, nutrients, moisture, and other ingredients beneficial to these cover crops.

When we were children, people took great pride in their work during every season. They had every right to celebrate their accomplishments, and we children were eager to join in.

We celebrated Labor Day as the symbolic end of summer. Most of us knew little about the holiday itself. We had heard that it was not fashionable to wear white or seersucker after Labor Day, but we were not fashion conscious enough to worry much about that. We knew that the holiday was celebrated the first Monday in September, but not that it was established as an official holiday in 1887. We never thought much about it as a celebration of the American labor movement or as a yearly national tribute to workers who made contributions to the well-being of their country.

We saw it as a day that marked the ending of those hot summer days and nights of freedom and set us up for the opening of another school year. Gone were the Sundays of "all day singing and dinner on the ground" at church and the weekdays of digging worms and visiting favorite fishing holes. Labor Day was the last hurrah before we went back to work. We made the most of the parade or picnic or town celebration, carefully planned by our local citizens as a labor of love. We never connected Labor Day to anything scary.

Roberta's Uncle Lawrence often came to visit around Labor Day. He usually stayed until the first good cold spell so he would be with the family at hog killing time to share the "fresh meat" that Roberta's mother and grandmother cooked so well.

Uncle Lawrence was a most welcomed storyteller. He told the family this haunting Labor Day story and swore it was true. Of course, he is also the one who told Roberta that the Bogey Man lived under her bed. Roberta couldn't tell if that was the truth or not because she was always afraid to look! You'll need to decide that one for yourself.

Here is Roberta's version of the story that her Uncle Lawrence told her.

Uncle Lawrence told us that he had been down to Adair County to visit his brother George for several days just after Labor Day. Uncle George had business with a farmer way out in the country, so Uncle Lawrence rode along. While Uncle George was talking to the man—Mr. Foley, I think he said was the man's name—at the side of the yard, Uncle Lawrence struck up a conversation with two teenage boys who were sitting in the yard. He sat on a stump beside them.

"Did you go to the Labor Day doings in town this year?" he asked them. "Guess they had a parade and a street fair, huh?"

The boys nodded yes, but didn't give any details.

"What happened? Didn't you have a good time?" Uncle Lawrence persisted.

Before the boys could answer, Uncle George and Mr. Foley came back to where the boys and Lawrence were sitting.

"Haven't you boys got some chores to do?" Mr. Foley asked.

"Yes, sir," they said in unison, nodded good-bye, and left the yard, heading toward the barn without answering Uncle Lawrence's question.

"I was just making conversation with your boys," Uncle Lawrence commented. "I asked them about Labor Day, but they didn't look like they had much fun. That used to be a big thing when I was a boy. There were booths for games and displays, lots of good food, and then the parade. I guess things have changed."

"Nah," said Mr. Foley. "They just got a little scare Monday before they went to town. Something strange happened and none of us can explain it. They swear it was true."

"What's strange around here?" Uncle George grinned. "I thought nothing ever happened out this way."

"I'm serious," said Mr. Foley. "The boys had been putting off doing the fall plowing. I finally had to tell them that the little field over by the garden had to be plowed before they could go to the Labor Day celebration. They grumbled, but finally got started fairly early. They are kind of sweet on Milton Alley's girls and they had plans to meet them in town before the parade. Milton approved. He said many a time that he loved his girls, but wished he had some boys. He seemed to look kindly on my two as suitors for his daughters."

"I always thought the socializing was the best part of Labor Day," Uncle Lawrence said. "That should have made them enjoy going in to town."

"Well," Mr. Foley continued, "they were discouraged because they didn't think they were going to get through plowing in time to go. Then they heard Milton holler from the fence and ask them why they weren't in town. They told him they had orders from me to plow the field, but it was taking a long time. Milton turned and walked away and the boys kept plowing. In a little while, they looked up and saw Milton with his old mule, Ronald, hitched to the plow. He was plowing on the other side of the field. It gave them new hope when they saw they had help. They worked as hard as they could, stopping only when they absolutely had to have a break. They noticed that Milton kept right on plowing without stopping to take a rest. In what seemed like no time, the three finished plowing the whole field. The boys thanked Milton for helping them finish so quickly and took off to get ready to go to town. Milton only nodded and went back home with old Ronald. He always was a good-hearted man."

"What was so strange about that?" Uncle Lawrence asked him.

"Hold on! I'm getting there!" Mr. Foley continued. "When the boys got to town they couldn't find Milton's girls. They were pretty ticked off at me at that point for making them miss seeing the girls. They decided to get something to eat, and they asked the man in the booth if he had seen the girls."

"It's not likely they would be here in view of what happened," he said. "Their pa, Milton, died of a heart attack late Sunday night."

"Oh, I see," Uncle George interrupted. "I guess the boys *were* shook up if he died Sunday night and helped them plow Monday morning!"

"Are you sure they didn't see someone else and just thought it was Milton?" asked Uncle Lawrence.

"No way," said Mr. Foley. "They talked to him. And nobody could mistake that old mule Ronald."

Uncle Lawrence and Uncle George drove back home, and Uncle Lawrence looked at the fields and fences around him, normal-looking as always, and found it hard to believe what had happened.

"Just imagine," he told us. "A dead man and a live mule teamed up to help two young people go have some fun on Labor Day. I'd have to call that a labor of love!"

The Ghost That Hated Labor Day

Most people love holidays. We assumed that ghosts do, too, but we learned that this is not true from a story Roberta tells about her sister.

My sister Fatima and her husband, Ervin, bought an old house in Kentucky near the Tennessee state line. It had every appearance of being their dream house. A little stream ran in front of some woods behind a big sloping backyard where my nephew and his friends could play.

Ervin's job took him to Tennessee, and the family felt lucky to find this house on such short notice. They moved into their new home in August, and immediately noticed some strange things happening in the house.

At first they heard the door from the garage open, followed by footsteps going into the bedroom next to the garage. They always checked, but found nobody in the house except the family.

Next, they found a pair of men's work shoes in the closet in that bedroom where the footsteps went. The shoes were worn and had traces of mud on the soles. They were placed neatly side by side.

"Where did these come from?" asked Fatima.

"I don't know," said Ervin. "They aren't mine."

They asked their son, but he had no idea where they came from. None of his new friends had been in the house the day before to play a trick like that.

The next day, when they looked in the closet, the shoes were gone! Only small crumbles of mud remained on the closet floor.

The third thing that happened was that they heard wheezing and choking sounds coming from what they now jokingly called "the haunted bedroom." It definitely sounded like a male.

On Labor Day, the weird happenings all came to a head.

It was stormy that night. Clouds rolled in at dusk and took over the sunny sky that had been so perfect for the day's activities. Fatima and Ervin had taken my nephew to a Labor Day parade, but they had made it home before the storm came in.

As the storm roared across the sky, the outside door slammed and footsteps stomped like someone wearing work shoes into the bedroom. This time, it sounded so much like a real person that they all went to check. The room was empty, so they turned to go.

The bedroom door slammed behind them, and loud choking sounds and wheezing began, like someone struggling for breath. Then the storm ceased and the sounds stopped. It was quiet for the rest of the night, but the silence was too eerie for the family to sleep much.

The next morning, Fatima made a decision to check into the history of the house they had bought. When her son left for school and her husband left for work, she left for the library.

The local librarian was a friendly, helpful woman, so Fatima introduced herself and the two struck up a conversation.

"So you bought the old Tucker place?" the librarian said.

"Yes," said Fatima, "but we don't know the history of the place. Do you know anything about it?"

"Well, I don't know that I could tell you much," she said.

"Anything you could tell me would help," said Fatima. "You see, there are some things about the house that we can't explain."

Fatima decided to tell the librarian about everything that had happened. Oddly enough, the woman didn't seem shocked.

"Mr. Tucker was a hardworking man," she said. "After his wife died, he only had a nephew who lived somewhere in Tennessee. Mr. Tucker planted a garden every year, and he usually had everything harvested and the soil dug up by Labor Day. He always got upset if he didn't get his work done."

"We thought he might have been sick," said Fatima.

"He was at the end," said the librarian.

"Do you think he has come back to haunt the house?" asked Fatima. "Doesn't he want us there?"

"I wouldn't want to say this publicly," said the librarian, "because some people get all upset when ghosts are mentioned, but I think he comes back every year to finish digging up his last garden."

"Have other people experienced this haunting?" asked Fatima.

"Well, I have heard stories, but not many talk about it," the librarian answered.

"Please tell me all you know," Fatima said.

"It's a sad story," the librarian began. "Mr. Tucker's health began to fail a year before he died, but he was determined to put out his garden like always. It was on the land in back of that strip of woods, a good way from the house.

"Mr. Tucker got to feeling so bad that he finally had to go to the doctor. The doctor told him he had a serious heart problem. The doctor told him he needed to forget about gardening and have surgery.

"Mr. Tucker would have none of that. Every time he came to town, everybody could tell he was struggling to breathe. He was wheezing and choking for air all the time.

"Labor Day came, and Mr. Tucker told his neighbor he

was about finished with the digging in the garden. He was so happy he was going to meet his deadline.

"'I hate to leave a job half done,' he said. 'I always liked to set deadlines for myself and meet them.'

"Then a storm came up unexpectedly and Mr. Tucker had to quit and go to the house. That night, the strain of all he had been doing caught up with him. His heart gave out and he died in his bedroom by the garage.

"When his neighbor didn't see him outside the next morning, he went to check and found him dead.

"Now don't quote me on this, but I think he hates Labor Day. I think his ghost comes back to finish his work each year, and I think that is what you heard."

Fatima promised she would not tell anyone where she got her information, except for her husband and son.

Ervin and the young son were surprised that Fatima had found out so much about the happenings related to their new house. They looked at the land behind the house, but it was overgrown with weeds. They had it mowed, but didn't plant anything there.

The year went by uneventfully—until late August came again. Once again, they heard the door opening and footsteps going to the bedroom. This time, they decided to take some action that might prevent another dramatic Labor Day night.

Ervin had the small field plowed again, but this time he also had the soil turned over. He thought that, this way, perhaps Mr. Tucker would feel as though his work was done and not come back this year. Maybe he would be able to find peace on the other side.

The family waited to see what would happen.

Nothing did! The footsteps, opening doors, and choking and wheezing ceased. They worried a little about Labor Day, especially when a storm came up just before dark and dumped rain all night. Still, nothing unusual happened.

After that, Mr. Tucker never paid a visit again. Fatima and her family, however, wondered if he still hated Labor Day!

Dare

The men in the Simpson family hunted for food, but they did not hunt as a sport. Their targets were opossums, rabbits, squirrels, quail, wild turkeys, and an occasional wild duck. All these supplemented the food they raised on the farm, including hogs and chickens.

To aid in the hunting, Roberta's Uncle Josh kept hunting dogs. His best hunter and most faithful companion was a mixed-breed dog he called Dare. Though Dare unquestionably recognized Uncle Josh as his master, he was fond of the rest of the family, too.

Most farmers had dogs to help out. They often worked from dawn to dusk to tend their crops of corn and other grain, tobacco, and vegetables, and even hired out to other farmers or swapped work to reap their harvests. The people in the neighborhood helped each other when help was needed—except for one man whom they called Old Bunker.

Old Bunker worked now and then to get a little spending money, but mostly he liked to lie in his bunk and smoke his roll-your-own cigarettes. He always seemed to find money to buy the supply of whiskey that he consumed daily. People figured that he stole most of it.

One night Uncle Josh and some friends decided to go possum hunting. They took their dogs and set out into the woods behind Uncle Josh's farm. They had walked quite a way when the dogs treed something. The men followed the sound of the dogs; but when they got there, they found only quivering dogs, with no sign of Dare or the prey the dogs had been chasing. Uncle Josh called and called, but this time Dare didn't come.

For days, Uncle Josh went out looking for his dog, but he never found a sign of where she might be. Though he knew it was very unlikely, he hoped that Dare was just lost and would find her way home.

Labor Day came, and Uncle Josh went into town to get some supplies. Aunt Marie and Grandma Simpson stayed home to shell some beans for supper. The weather was still warm, so they sat on the front porch to do their work.

It wasn't long before they were surprised to see a man coming down the road. They weren't scared because it was a common thing to see neighbors walking.

"He's turning down the lane," said Aunt Marie. "I wonder why he would be coming here. Since Josh just left, he must have seen him along the road."

As he came closer, Grandma Simpson recognized him.

"Why, that's Old Bunker!" she said. "I guess he knows Josh sold some of the crops and is coming to ask for money."

"He looks like he has been drinking," said Marie. "He's weaving a little as he walks."

"Josh home?" he asked, walking right up to the porch.

"No," said Aunt Marie. "I'm surprised you didn't see him on the road. He just left."

Old Bunker grinned slightly. Grandma Simpson did not like it.

"You ladies here alone?" he asked.

Without waiting for them to answer, he stepped up onto the porch.

Grandma Simpson and Aunt Marie did not scare easily, but there was something about the way Old Bunker was acting that put them on alert. If men came to a home and the man of the house was gone, the visitors would leave. They never came to sit with the women. They never discussed business with the women.

"I heard Josh did good with the crop sales," Old Bunker said. "I thought he might spare me a little money."

"You'd have to talk to him about that," said Grandma Simpson. "I think you'd better go on along now and come back later."

"I think it would be better if you gave me some of that money now," said Old Bunker, standing up and walking toward the two women. He reached into his pocket and pulled out an old hunting knife.

The women had no weapons within reach. If Grandma

Simpson had only had her rifle by her, she would have shot him in a heartbeat, but she didn't.

"Let's go inside," he said to them, motioning to the door.

Suddenly, from around the corner of the house, came a dog, growling and snarling. It was Dare! She lunged toward Old Bunker and knocked the knife to the floor. Grandma Simpson snatched it up, but Old Bunker didn't stay around to notice. Trying to fight off the dog, he jumped from the porch, staggered, regained his balance, and ran down the lane toward the road. The two women looked back at Dare, but she had vanished.

When Josh came home and learned what had happened, he went for the sheriff. Old Bunker had cleared out, though, and he never came back. We heard that he was killed in a car wreck near the Ohio state line while he was headed for Cincinnati.

Dare never came back, either. She had come home to defend her human family and, when that was accomplished, she went back into the spirit world.

Roberta always believed that Old Bunker had killed Dare and that she came back to get revenge.

Grandma Simpson had always looked at Labor Day as just another day, but this was one Labor Day she would remember and celebrate. She and Aunt Marie always wondered what would have happened if Dare had not returned to drive Old Bunker away.

Ridge Dancer

In the Brown family, the children always looked up to their parents, grandparents, and other older people to explain mysteries to them. A neighbor who had once lived in the foothills of the Appalachian Mountains told one mystery to Lonnie's family, but he never had the solution to the mystery he shared.

This is how Lonnie tells that story.

It was a warm Labor Day night, and our family and a neighbor, who had come to sit with us until bedtime, had taken chairs outside to enjoy a refreshing breeze. The moonlight was bright, and the sky was clear except for the faraway stars.

"Tonight reminds me of the Ridge Dancer," our visitor said.

He had our attention right away.

"A Ridge Dancer?" asked my brother. "What is that?"

"I am not sure I can answer that," he said. "It was a silent figure, but it danced like it was hearing drums beating."

He told us then that his family had once bought a small farm in a valley beneath a high Appalachian ridge that had an open spot cleared on top among the trees. The family went up to explore, but the clearing looked like any other field.

"It seemed like a hard place to reach in order to cultivate, but obviously someone had made the effort," our visitor said. "It wasn't our land, though, so it wasn't our concern. We went on home and tended to our own business."

He said they had moved to their farm in early spring, so they planted and harvested crops the first year.

From time to time during the spring and summer, they would climb the ridge and check out the clearing.

"It was odd, but nothing was growing in the clearing except short grass," he said. "It didn't look like anyone had been there to cut back bushes and weeds or mow the grass. It always remained the same."

"What was the clearing for on a ridge?" asked my brother.

"Well," said our neighbor, "there is a story about that ridge. They say it was sacred to the Indians. Their medicine man would dance on the ridge on the night of Labor Day if there were going to be good crops the next year. "

"Why did he do that?" my brother wanted to know. "And why on Labor Day?"

"That's the mystery, son," the neighbor said. "Nobody really knows. There were a lot of Indians here when Kentucky was first settled. From their camps on both sides of the ridge, they would have a good view of anything that happened on the ridge top.

"The medicine man performed his magic to find out how things would grow the next year, and then he danced on top of the ridge to let them know whether food would be plentiful the next year, or if they should move on."

"I never heard any Indian stories like that," said my brother.

"I hadn't either," said our neighbor. "I am just telling you what I know about the Ridge Dancer."

"Did you see him?" my brother asked.

"Yes," replied the neighbor. "We saw him the fall after we moved there. It was Labor Day, and we were relaxing in the yard after supper, just like we are now. All of a sudden, the moon got brighter. We looked up and saw a figure dancing on the ridge! Just like the story says, we had a good crop the next year."

"Did you ever see him again?" asked my brother, who was really hooked on the story now.

"No," our neighbor answered. "We watched for him the next Labor Day, but he never came."

"Did you have a bad harvest the next year?" my brother asked.

"Yes, the harvest was bad. We barely made it through the winter," said our neighbor. "My dad sold the farm and we moved here. I never went back. I sometimes think of the Ridge Dancer, though, and wonder who he was and if he is still dancing."

Columbus Day

Columbus Day first became a federal holiday in the United States in 1937, instituted by President Franklin D. Roosevelt. Since 1970 it has been celebrated on the second Monday in October. The holiday commemorates the anniversary of Italian navigator Christopher Columbus's arrival in the Americas on October 12, 1492.

Columbus Day celebrations tend to be more about Italian American heritage than the man himself.

Columbus Day is celebrated in several other countries besides the United States, though the extent of the festivities ranges from large-scale parades to nonobservance.

If it hadn't been for Columbus Day, we would not have had the following holiday ghost story.

Columbus Day Ghost

Roberta tells this story about a sleepover she had one October night when she was young.

I rarely had more than one friend sleep over at a time, but on this occasion my mother, Lillian Simpson, gave me permission to have one friend and three of my cousins spend the night.

It was October, so the air was just right for sitting outside on the porch. After Mom and Dad went to bed, we moved closer into a tight circle and began to tell stories.

My cousins and I told each other stories all the time, so we had heard very few new ones to tell each other. That's why we were eager to hear stories from my friend. This girl and I knew each other from school, but she lived all the way over in the next town, so she had a new territory of tales for us to explore.

"Do you know any family stories?" I asked. "You know, scary or strange?"

"I know one about my sister," she replied, "and it is absolutely true."

"What happened?" one of my cousins asked.

"My sister never would have seen a ghost if it hadn't been for Columbus Day," she said.

"A ghost story? Great! Tell us about it!" we said.

"My sister worked for the post office in Taylor County," she said. "She had the day off because Columbus Day was a holiday for them. She was watching for her neighbor to come home from school so she could see if she wanted to go to dinner and a movie.

"Her neighbor always complained because schools remained open on Columbus Day and she had to work. She didn't think anyone should celebrate Columbus Day because she knew there were other people in America before he showed up.

"She saw her neighbor drive in a little later than usual. She realized she had stopped for some groceries when she saw her take the brown grocery bag out of the car.

"My sister called to the neighbor from the kitchen door and asked her to call as soon as she got the groceries put away. The neighbor nodded and went on inside.

"She had lived alone since her mother had died a few weeks ago, and she often mentioned that she missed the comfort of having another person live in the house.

"My sister waited several minutes, but her neighbor didn't call. She thought maybe she had received a call and was tied up on the phone. She waited a few more minutes and tried to call her. The phone rang and rang. The line wasn't busy; there simply was no answer.

"My sister thought that maybe her neighbor had simply forgotten to call, but that didn't seem likely. It was Columbus Day, though, and the neighbor wasn't used to my sister's being home before she was.

"When my sister hung up the phone, she looked out the window to see if she could see her neighbor. She was surprised to see an older lady at the neighbor's window beckoning to her. If she hadn't known the mother was dead, she would have thought it was the old lady. Who could it be?

"My sister quickly ran to her neighbor's house. The door was open, so she cautiously went inside.

"She looked around the room and noticed something first thing that unnerved her very much.

"The brown paper bag filled with groceries sat on the kitchen table. It was still upright, but the celery had fallen out. The melting ice cream had turned the paper dark brown as it soaked through the bag. It had run down the back of the chair, dripped off, and mingled with the pool of blood on the floor. Then she saw her neighbor by the blood pool, unconscious and barely breathing.

"My sister was shocked at the sight and then immediately afraid that the intruder might still be in the house. She stood perfectly still, but there was no other sound or movement that she could hear.

"Still, she knew she had to get help for her friend right away, so she dialed for help from the phone in the kitchen.

"While she waited, my sister kept listening for any sounds in the rest of the house. There weren't any. The intruder must have grabbed her neighbor's purse and run off. Maybe her phone call had scared him off. Maybe the old woman had scared him off. Whatever the reason, my sister was certainly thankful he was gone.

"In the commotion that followed, my sister forgot about the reason she went over to her neighbor's house to check on her. She rode to the hospital with her neighbor and stayed there until the doctor came out and said she would be all right.

"When her neighbor had recovered and come home, the two were talking about that afternoon. The neighbor asked why my sister had come over.

"My sister said, 'I saw an older lady motioning to me from your window. It looked just like your mother! I guess it was her ghost, because no old woman was there when I arrived.'

"The neighbor laughed and said, 'You and Columbus have something in common. He wasn't the first to discover America and you weren't the first to discover me! You both had help from other people.'

"My sister said, 'Other people? What do you mean?'

"The neighbor said, 'You just told me yourself. You said an older lady motioned for you to come over. Obviously, my mother's ghost found me first.'

"It made them both feel a little spooky, but they were glad to know that the dear old lady was still around."

Halloween

Halloween is celebrated on October 31, but it did not become a holiday in the United States until the nineteenth century. The traditions of the Puritans still lingered, and this restricted the observance of many holidays, including Halloween.

Then nearly two million Irish immigrated to the United States after the Irish Potato Famine (1845–1849). They brought with them their heritage of Irish legends and Halloween. Scottish immigrants to Canada and the United States brought their own version of Halloween.

Many celebrated the holiday with home parties centered on children's activities, but outside pranks and mischief became common as well.

Children began going door-to-door receiving treats (thus reducing tricks), and what became known as "trick-or-treating" had become a widespread custom by the 1950s. Manufacturers began producing masks, costumes, and yard decorations such as jack-o'-lanterns, scarecrows, witches, foam tombstones, and lots of other scary-looking things.

Halloween is now the second most popular holiday (after Christmas) for decorating in the United States.

In many places, trick-or-treaters are welcomed by lit porch lights and jack-o'-lanterns. If the porch light is off, it is a signal for the trick-or-treaters not to stop at that house. Because some people choose to harm trick-or-treaters, it is now becoming a trend to have trick-or-treating confined to set hours and supervised events at malls, firehouses, or other safe places.

Some people do not recognize Halloween for religious reasons, and some object to the commercialism now connected with the holiday, but most people celebrate Halloween as a time for fun.

Halloween is the perfect time to share scary stories like the following.

Graveyard Pumpkins

We were always cautioned not to take dirt from graveyards because it would bring bad luck. We never challenged this warning, so we had no way of knowing if bad luck really would result. We did hear of one story so strange that it was hard to believe, but those in the area close to the Smith Woods in Adair County swore it really happened.

Lonnie tells this story about a graveyard near the Smith Woods.

When I was a boy, Mom and Dad moved our family to the edge of the Smith Woods, where an old graveyard had a boundary in common with a field about a half-mile or so down the road from our house.

There were all sorts of tales told about those woods. Babies were heard crying near a branch, but a search would turn up no evidence of anyone being there. Some said spirits lived in the trees and that they would wail when a storm was coming or when men brought saws to cut them down. It was also believed that one should "knock on wood" (the trunks or limbs) when passing the trees so they would know you were friendly and meant them no harm. Being in the tree's good graces meant that no bad luck would come to the knocker.

Inside the woods were open patches and the remains of an old dirt road that had been worn down to leave banks on each side. Huge, mouthwatering dewberries grew on vines along these banks, and one could stand in the road and pick the berries.

My mother and her sisters were picking berries there one day when they heard horses and a wagon approaching. They could even hear the harness jangling and the horses snorting. They climbed the bank and waited for them to pass, but nothing ever appeared. There were many reports of mysterious sounds of riders in the woods, too, but nothing was ever seen.

The Sinclair family owned the house and the field that joined the old cemetery near us. They had two children, and we quickly became friends.

As Halloween drew near, we began to make plans on

how we would celebrate. When we asked where we could buy some pumpkins for jack-o'-lanterns, the Sinclair children looked faintly disturbed and said we would have to buy them in town. In fact, they said they had not had any jack-o'-lanterns for several years. Curious about why they didn't, we urged them to tell us the reason.

Finally, the Sinclair boy told us. Several years ago, when they were about six and seven, their father had some pumpkins growing in the back of their field, and he told the children to go gather two pumpkins for their jack-o'-lanterns.

When they got to the back of the field, they could see that a pumpkin vine had grown over the boundary into the graveyard. That vine had pumpkins that looked bigger and were a brighter orange than the pumpkins in their field, so the children stepped into the graveyard, picked two big pumpkins, and took them home. They had been told not to take things growing in the graveyard, but this vine was growing from their field and the pumpkins were just sitting on the graveyard dirt—not growing from it.

The children said nothing to their parents about where they had gotten the pumpkins. They cleaned out the insides of their pumpkins and carved smiling faces on them. Then they placed them on the porch and left to go trick-or-treating.

When they returned, they were shocked and frightened by what they saw. The faces on their jack-o'-lanterns had changed! They were now wearing expressions of pain instead of happiness. The children looked closer, but they couldn't figure out how the original carvings could have been altered or who would have done it. If it hadn't been a prankster, then it had to have been a spirit!

"Did you get these pumpkins from our field like I told you?" asked Mr. Sinclair.

His look was stern, and they knew they couldn't get away with lying to him. They confessed that they had gotten them from the graveyard.

Without a word, he took the two jack-o'-lanterns to the back of the field and smashed them on the graveyard vine.

When he got back to the house, he ordered the children to go to their rooms without their treats.

"Mark my words," he said when they objected. "There will be consequences worse than this."

A week passed, and the consequences came. Grandma and Grandpa Sinclair came down with the flu. The local doctor treated them, but he couldn't save them. When the Sinclair children saw their grandparents just before the old folks died, they noticed that both had expressions of pain on their faces just like the faces on the pumpkins.

When we heard that story, we understood why the Sinclair children had not wanted any jack-o'-lanterns on Halloween.

Halloween Hut

Noel, a school friend of ours, lived with his family near Paducah many years ago when he was a boy. He told us a story of a very memorable Halloween he spent there.

There were only two other boys who lived near him. Since they went to the same school, they became friends. They didn't have much to do for fun out in the country, so they were wondering how to celebrate Halloween.

The kids who lived in town talked about the parties they were having and the costumes they were wearing to go door-to-door trick-or-treating. There were only a few houses in the country, so Noel and his friends didn't think it would be very profitable to go door-to-door there.

"Why don't we dress up and go to town to trick-or-treat?" suggested Noel.

His two friends agreed, and the three started planning their costumes. They decided the easiest thing would be to go as cowboys, so they got their costumes ready before checking with their parents.

Noel's parents were not sure that it would be a good idea to go into town on this particular Halloween night. Dark clouds crept in unnoticed until a rumble of thunder called attention to the large bank that had formed.

"Son," said Noel's father, "I think it is going to be raining in a couple of hours. I don't want you caught out in a storm."

"I've made some cookies," said Noel's mother. "You boys could stay here and play games."

"We could do that after we go trick-or-treating," said Noel. "They give out lots of candy in town. Couldn't you drop us off, Dad? We could get our treats and have time to walk home."

Reluctantly, Noel's father drove them to town.

"Do you want me to come back and get you in an hour?" he asked.

"No!" all the boys answered.

"Okay," he said, "but keep an eye on the clouds."

Even as Noel's father said this, the boys were already off, hurrying down the street to ring doorbells. Clouds were not on their minds. Wherever they went, they got lots of candy and chewing gum.

They were at the end of the last street when they heard it.

KABOOM!

The thunder rattled windows in houses and scared the boys into heading home as fast as they could go. A wind had picked up, and leaves swirled around them as they ran.

"We're never going to make it," said Noel.

"Let's take the shortcut through the woods," said one of the boys, leading the other two off the road through the trees. "There used to be an old hut in here. Maybe we can find shelter."

Breathless from running, they broke into a clearing and saw the old hut in the middle. It looked deserted and dilapidated; but as they approached, the door opened and an old man motioned them inside.

"This is going to be a bad storm, boys. You'll be safe here," he said.

The boys and the old man did not try to carry on a conversation because the storm was too loud for them to hear each other. Lightning bolts struck trees nearby, and hail the size of golf balls hit the ground around the hut. The rain sounded like a tap dancer on the roof. The boys thought the storm was going to last forever!

Finally, the rain let up and the clouds moved on. The boys thanked the old man and left. He only smiled and nodded.

As the boys reached the road, they met Noel's father and the fathers of the other two boys, who were out looking for them.

"Where have you been?" Noel's father asked. "We drove through town and all along the road, but we couldn't find you!"

"We took the shortcut and found shelter with the old man in the hut in the woods," Noel explained.

"That's impossible," said one of the fathers. "The old man was killed in a storm a couple of years ago. That old hut has been locked up ever since!"

The boys were adamant about what they saw. The fathers decided to show them they were wrong, so they all went to the hut in the woods.

When they reached the door, the boys couldn't believe what they were seeing. A padlock and cobwebs were on the door. It was obvious that nobody had been inside.

The boys insisted that the old man had opened the door and let them in.

"Maybe you're right after all," said Noel's father. "Look at the ground."

They all looked and were amazed by what they saw.

Three sets of footprints made by the boys clearly led away from the door!

Did the old man come back from the other side to save the boys from the kind of death he had? They didn't know. They only knew that they all saw the old man and that they would never forget him.

The Star Theater

Almost every Halloween, we go back to our hometown, Russell Springs, Kentucky, to join our friends, author Irene Black and her husband, Ford Nash, to do a Halloween show (*The Ghosts of Russell County*), with all the proceeds collected from the event going to the public library. The event is held at the Star Theater at 546 Main Street in Russell Springs. Every year, there is a wonderful turnout to support the library.

Construction started on the Star Theater on May 2, 1949, by a Mr. A. V. Lutrell. It opened on February 28, 1950, with the movie *Mrs. Mike,* staring Dick Powell and Evelyn Keyes. Roberta's class attended that first movie as a field trip, and she still remembers how excited she was to get home and tell her family how much she loved it. The theater had a special place in Roberta's heart from the very first day.

The Star Theater thrilled audiences for three decades. The two of us and our friends loved the Saturday afternoon serials (mostly westerns), which always ended in cliffhangers that lured us back the next Saturday to see what happened.

Once the theater was showing a comedy that Roberta

wanted to see. Our neighbor had a car, so he made several trips to take carloads of us to town. He'd let one load out and then go back for another.

Considering all the feelings associated with the Star Theater, it is little wonder that it is haunted.

After the theater closed in the 1970s, the building was used as furniture stores, clothing stores, and even a restaurant and disco, but none of these businesses stayed very long. Many people just came and went.

Then, in the early 1990s, the Star Theater was renovated and was reopened in July 1994 by the Russell County Arts Council. Since then, hundreds of shows have been staged there very successfully.

More than one person has reported seeing the ghosts of one of three different people who cared deeply for the theater before they died.

Two of our personal acquaintances, both totally sane and levelheaded, have seen the ghost of a young man. In one account, the apparition was seen on stage and out in the lobby. In another, he floated just above the floor in front of the curtains before the show started. It does not surprise us at all that anyone who was connected to the theater in any way might want to come back after death to visit the old theater over and over again.

The first year we did our Halloween program there, our friend let us in and then went back to get some things from the car. We heard a noise from the projection booth area and thought someone was up there looking at us. When we looked up, we saw nothing, but we still felt like we were being watched. At the time, we assumed that someone else with a key had come inside to set up something for the program.

Now, when we go in early on Halloween to set up, we still have the distinct feeling of being watched, even though we know nobody else is there.

On May 17, 2014, we went to the Star Theater with our friends, Sharon Brown (a ghost hunter) and Irene Black and Ford Nash (authors of books of "haints" and mystery). With them, we encountered some paranormal activity in the aisle on the left side of the theater. A rehearsal was in progress on the stage, so we assumed that some ghostly presence was there, enjoying the performance.

Unknown Visitor

Lonnie tells this story about something that happened one Halloween when he was a boy.

A neighbor of ours, old man Edwards, had a cabin way back in the Smith Woods. He didn't come out often, but now and then he would stop by our house when he was on his way to pick up some supplies.

One day, shortly after Halloween, he arrived at our house one morning right after we had finished breakfast.

"I'd like to start a project right away," he said. "I want to finish it before bad weather sets in."

"Oh?" said Dad.

"I need your help, Mr. Brown," he said, "if you can spare the time."

"What do you need, Mr. Edwards?" Dad asked.

"I need you to haul some logs I've cut," he explained, "and I need you to help me build another wall around my cabin."

That sounded a bit odd to Dad. He had seen the old man's cabin, and it seemed quite solid. Dad never turned down extra work, though.

"I have time to help you out," Dad told him. "When do you want me to start?"

"Like I said, I'd like to start right away," he said. "I want the work finished before cold weather sets in. Something happened Halloween night that made me realize this needs to be done."

"What happened?" Dad asked.

"Mr. Brown, I don't scare easy, but there is something out there in those woods that paid me a visit on Halloween. I aim to be ready if it comes back again."

"What was it?" Dad asked him.

"To tell you the truth, I don't know. It was cloudy on Halloween this year, so it got dark a little earlier than usual. After I did my chores, I went inside and locked up. I fixed some supper and sat down to read awhile before going to bed.

"I missed the company of my old hunting dog, Boomer. He got out on the road and got killed by a truck last summer, you know."

"Yes," said Dad. "I remember. Sorry."

"I always kept him inside at night, so I never had to worry about anyone or anything sneaking up on me. He was a good watchdog.

"Well, anyway, I read until I began to get sleepy. I blew out the lamp and went on to bed. I was just dozing off when I heard something walking around outside. It crossed my mind that it was Halloween and that some boys from town might have come out to do some mischief, so I lay still to see if I could figure out what was going on.

"I could only hear one set of footsteps. As I listened, I ruled out a group of boys pulling a prank. This was something big—sounded bigger than a human, like an animal—but it was walking on two legs. I admit that I wished with all my heart that Boomer was with me.

"The thing came right up to the cabin. The smell was awful. I don't think it was a bear. It acted like it had human intelligence. It began to make this awful sound, sort of a cross between a howl and a growl. Then it began to pound on the walls and the doors. Then I heard this scratching at the front door. The thing got louder and louder, and so did the scratching. I got out of bed and tried to peek out the window, but it was too dark to see anything.

"Then suddenly it stopped and I heard it going away. The scratching stopped, too. I looked down and couldn't believe what I was seeing. There were scratches inside on the door. If I believed in ghosts, I'd think Boomer came back to help me."

"Did you see any tracks the next morning?" asked Dad

"The grass had been trampled down, but no track was distinct. I have a feeling it will come back again, and I am not sure that my old cabin will hold together."

"When would you like me to start?" Dad asked the old man.

"How about day after tomorrow?" he said. "I think I can have all the supplies ready by then."

"That's fine," Dad told him. "I'll be there at sunup so we can get an early start."

"Good," said Mr. Edwards.

He walked away, and that was the last time we ever saw him.

The sheriff came by the next morning asking if Dad knew anything about old man Edwards.

"A hunter was going by the Edwards cabin at daybreak, and he saw the door off on the front porch and some other damage to the cabin walls. He checked, but old man Edwards wasn't there. The hunter came to town and told me. I went out to the cabin, but there is no sign of Edwards. There is quite a bit of damage to the cabin, but no blood or evidence that he was injured. I'm getting up a search party to help my deputy and me look."

Dad told him about Mr. Edwards's visit to us the day before, and the strange story he told.

The sheriff was as puzzled as Dad. They had never heard about anything like that in the woods.

Dad and some of the other neighbor men went off with

the sheriff and deputy to look for the old man. They searched all of the Smith Woods, but never found a trace of him.

Mr. Edwards had no family, so the sheriff simply put the door back on its hinges and boarded up all the damaged places on the cabin.

After that, none of us ever went alone to that cabin, and none of us wanted to be in that area alone—especially on Halloween.

Stone Unturned

Lonnie has another story about Halloween in the area of the Smith Woods.

On Halloween, we boys didn't have a lot to do in the country. We confined our mischief to harmless things, like putting brush in the middle of country roads or taking the bells off the cows and running through cornfields, ringing them so farmers would think their cows were in the corn.

A couple of hills over, however, two young men, who were probably in their late teens or early twenties, were doing more harmful things. Huston and Billy Ray never had a job, and they became very skilled in stealing.

People locked their smokehouses at night unless they wanted to risk a missing ham in the morning. Sometimes, if Huston and Billy Ray were desperate for food, they would break into a henhouse and steal some chickens and eggs before the squawking of the chickens brought their owner running out with a gun. Normally, though, this was too risky.

Huston and Billy Ray were considered good-for-nothings, but they weren't fools. They knew not to bother homes where men had their guns loaded and waiting. They especially liked to harass Widow Clark, who lived down the road from us.

Widow Clark was a frail-looking lady, but she managed to keep her farm going after her husband died. She couldn't do her own hog killing, but neighbors pitched in and helped her with things she couldn't do for herself. She owned a shotgun, but it wasn't in her nature to shoot to kill anyone. She had no lock on her smokehouse, so it was an easy target for Huston and Billy Ray. The boys thought it was funny to see Widow Clark come running out with her gun when she heard them prowling. Finally, the neighbor men got involved, put a lock on her smokehouse door, and had a word of warning for the would-be thieves.

Widow Clark took great pride in her herb garden. She especially loved the stone statue of an angel that stood right in the middle. Her husband had bought it for her years ago, and it had taken two men to put it in place. It was good they got it positioned to suit her, because it was too heavy for her to move herself.

She grew herbs in her garden that made her cooking tasty and cured most common ailments. She shared these generously with anyone who needed them.

Since her neighbors were so good to her, Widow Clark

tried to return the favor by helping them any way she could. She was always happy to sit up with someone who was sick so the rest of the family could get some sleep.

Then Widow Clark got sick herself. Her heart simply gave out, and nothing could be done to help her. She died quietly at home one Halloween night with neighbors at her bedside.

Halloween, of course, was the annual night for Huston and Billy Ray to go on the prowl. They wanted to treat themselves to one of Widow Clark's hams, but more than that, they wanted to scare the old lady. That night, they planned to break in and steal her money.

They didn't know that Widow Clark was dead until they approached her house and saw all the people gathered inside.

Huston and Billy Ray were grown men, but they still pouted like children when they didn't get their way.

"We can't get away with a ham tonight," said Billy Ray. "We'll have to come back again later."

"Yeah," said Huston. "Maybe while they're burying her."

Thwarted, the childish young men felt they had to do something. They were standing right beside Widow Clark's herb garden when they both had the same idea.

"Let's turn the angel statue over!"

It took both of them pushing as hard as they could, but the statue eventually toppled. The sound brought out some of the people who were inside the house to see what had happened. No one came out to the garden because, in the darkness, they could not see what had made the noise.

Huston and Billy Ray stood still so nobody would see them, but then they couldn't move for another reason. They squinted to be sure of what they were seeing. A white mist was forming around the statue. Slowly it rose to its original standing position with nobody around to raise it.

"It's her ghost!" said Billy Ray.

"Let's get out of here!" cried Huston.

The men who had come outside saw them as they ran and gave chase. This time Huston and Billy Ray spent some time in jail for all their mischief.

Widow Clark was buried in the family graveyard. The neighbors thought it only proper that the widow and the statue be together. They carefully moved the statue of the angel and placed it between the graves of Widow Clark and her husband.

Time in jail and a dose of the supernatural changed Huston and Billy Ray. They gave up stealing and they both got honest jobs.

Autumn Apparitions

Roberta recalls Halloweens past from her childhood days.

Once we got past Labor Day, it felt as though one holiday fell on the heels of another. Our spirits lifted because these end-of-year holidays brought out real spirits, the spooky ones at Halloween and the inspiring ones at Thanksgiving. These holidays also brought the prospect of candy, chewing gum, and homemade goodies for trick-or-treaters at Halloween, and good food from a bountiful harvest for our Thanksgiving feast. We waited with delight for visits from relatives and friends.

On Halloween, neighbors usually gathered at someone's house and we played games, had treats, and told scary stories. The younger children carved pumpkins, bobbed for apples, and sometimes had a costume contest. The older boys would sometimes go out on their own to do a little mischief, like turn over an outhouse or lay a log across the road. Often they would hide and then come out to move the log when somebody couldn't get by. Naturally, they acted like someone else had done it.

The cold did not seem to bother us too much then. We liked to play hide-and-seek in the shocks of fodder that were tied up in the fields for the cattle to eat. We slid down haystacks when we could get away with it.

At night at that time of year, we told stories inside around the fire because it was too cold to sit outside. Storytellers were not "professional" then, but they were some of the most gifted we have ever heard. We also talked about superstitions that some scoffed at and others accepted as the gospel. There were unforgettable stories based on some of these superstitions.

Thanksgiving made us pause to reflect on our blessings. These were days of pumpkin and apple pies, vegetables and fresh-baked bread, and cured ham and fresh game, hunted only for the purpose of eating. The men were responsible for bringing home a wild turkey, and the women stayed up most of the night getting it ready for dinner the next day.

Some families set a place at the table for loved ones who had gone before, but all of us were mindful of how good life was and how blessed we were. We were not surprised when a spirit came to visit.

Some relatives from out of town could only come at Thanksgiving because they wanted to be with their immediate families at Christmas. The early presents they brought made the long, cold nights warm and happy. There were puzzles, card games like Old Maid and Authors, crayons and coloring books, and board games like Uncle Wiggily or checkers.

As each holiday approached, we all became eager for company. Grandma Simpson would sometimes open the door and look out if she heard a car coming.

Lonnie and I were in Russell County on business one Halloween, so I suggested that we drive back to Grandma Simpson's old farm, where I had been born. New owners lived there, but they gave us permission to look around as long as we wanted to.

It had been many years since I had been there, and the new owners had made many changes. The cherry tree that once stood at the turn of the lane was gone. The old house had been torn down, and a huge silo stood where the house had been. The fields where Dad planted crops were now fenced pastures with cattle roaming where I once played.

As I stood looking toward the place where I had spent so many happy hours, I suddenly felt very strange. The cherry tree was there, very near to me. The silo was gone, and the house was back. I could see the trees around the yard. Then, much to my amazement, the door opened and there was Grandma Simpson, standing in the door looking out, as though she had heard our car. I wanted to run to her and go inside that house again, but when I stepped forward, the vision was gone. I was standing by the pasture fence with a big-eyed cow mooing at me.

Did I really step back in time to take one last look at my first home? Were the powers of Halloween playing tricks on me? Did Grandma's ghost hear our car and come to greet us? I never could explain it. In any case, the memories were with me.

Memories are always with us, just as real as the experiences of the past. Remember, memories can haunt as well as people.

Bethlehem Church

Bethlehem Church is located between Russell Springs and Columbia, Kentucky, on Highway 80 in Russell County near the Adair County line. The church was built in the late 1800s and served the community for many, many years until its deteriorating condition required that the church be rebuilt in the early 2000s.

There is an old belief that if you save a piece of wood from a church that has been torn down to make way for another building, this piece is considered sacred and will bring good luck to your home. Usually, it is blessed by a prayer for protection, and supposedly it brings the owner the positive presence of all those from the past who came to the church.

Although we have been gone for many years from the old church, it will always have a special place in our hearts and memories. We were fortunate enough to get a piece of chestnut wood from the old church's foundation to keep in our home, and since then, we have been blessed with unusually good luck. If this old piece of wood could talk, we wonder what stories it could tell.

Both of our families attended the church, as did almost all the other people in the neighborhood. It was the religious and social center for the community.

There were Sunday meetings, prayer meetings during the week, revivals, baptisms at nearby Russell Creek when the weather was warm, and plays or special programs on holidays. For us, there was always a peaceful atmosphere that gave us a sense of a combination of the songs, feelings, prayers, and beliefs of those who had gone before.

One Halloween, we came to Russell Springs on business and went to visit the graves of our family members and put flowers on the graves. Looking back, we believe we encountered two of those long-ago people who came back to visit just as we did.

When we parked on the road that wound its way through the cemetery, we paused to enjoy the view in all directions. Nobody else was in sight. We weren't surprised by this, since there was a chilly wind that nipped at our fingers and noses. We were glad we had worn our heavy coats. We got out of the car and started placing the wreaths we had brought for our loved ones.

As we finished, we turned and saw a woman and little girl looking at a tombstone in the middle of the graveyard. We had no idea of when they had arrived because we had been focused on our own errand, but, since no car was in sight, we figured they must have walked in or been dropped off.

The woman was wearing a gray coat and scarf, and the little girl wore a blue coat with a red scarf. The woman's shoulders were hunched forward against the wind, and the little girl huddled close to the woman. It was odd that they had come visiting without any flowers. They never looked at us or acknowledged us in any way.

We turned back to put some flower boxes in our car trunk, and when we looked back, the two of them had gone! We had turned away for only a minute. We looked in all directions, but they were simply not there. No car was anywhere in sight. If the woman and girl were walking, we would have been able to see them. We were curious, so we walked to the area where we had seen them. Up close, we couldn't be certain which grave they had been visiting. But we were certain that for a moment, the veil had been lifted from the beyond to allow spirits to come and go on that cold autumn day.

Ghosts in Cemetery at Free Union Separate Baptist Church

Lonnie tells a Halloween story about a cemetery near another church.

Located in Adair County, a few miles from Bethlehem Church, the Free Union Separate Baptist Church stands by a cemetery that is said to be haunted. Roberta and I have been there many times because my grandparents, Milton and Zona Mae Rooks, my uncles, Ed and Charlie, and several other family members are buried there. It's a peaceful country location and suggests nothing ghostly. We have seen strange shadows near tombstones, but nothing that could not be explained.

My mother, Lena Brown, shared a story that she heard while she was visiting that cemetery one Halloween many years ago. She always went to visit the family graves when she came down from Louisville to visit relatives.

She was walking through the middle of the graveyard when she noticed that she was not alone.

Another visitor, a lady who said she was from Ohio, obviously had the same idea. She approached Mom and struck up a conversation.

"Have you seen anything strange at the far section of the graveyard in the last few minutes?" she asked.

"No," my mother said. "I haven't noticed anything unusual. I just got here, though, and I have just been looking for my family graves. Have you seen something?"

"Well," said the visitor, "I saw a man with a baby, and he just vanished. He had on a navy blue suit, and the baby was wrapped in a pink blanket. One minute they were there, and the next they were gone. I guess something must be wrong with my eyes."

"The sun can play tricks on us," Mom said.

She wondered if the woman was playing a trick on her because my mother had not seen anyone in the graveyard when she came in. Mom noticed that the woman was very pale, but she didn't think much about it.

Then the two women went their separate ways. Mom told us about the strange encounter, but we all let the story slip out of our minds.

Then, in 2000, Lynwood Montell wrote a more detailed account of the ghostly man and baby in his book *Ghosts across Kentucky,* published by the University Press of Kentucky. He told of a couple that in 1972 had witnessed the ghost of a man holding a baby. They said he wore a navy blue suit and the baby's blanket was pink. The man appeared to be in his fifties. The couple looked in the area where they had seen the ghost and found a tombstone of a man in his fifties and one beside it belonging to a baby with the same last name as the man.

We have seen brief accounts of this haunting on websites now, but nobody knows the identity of the man or the little baby he is holding close. Maybe he and the baby are waiting for the baby's mother to join them.

On a visit to the cemetery recently, we found two graves close to each other. One was the grave of a male adult. The other was the grave of an infant. Could their spirits have been the ones visiting among the living on that long-ago Halloween Day?

Halloween House

Many stories support some of the superstitions that we talk about in our neighborhood storytelling sessions. As we mentioned earlier, it was considered bad luck to remove dirt from a graveyard; it was also considered bad luck to live in a house next to one. One family Roberta heard about scoffed at this idea and lived to regret it.

Here is her story.

Uncle Lawrence told us about this family during one of his visits. He and my Aunt Lily were living in a house in south central Kentucky, two houses down from a cemetery by a little country church.

An empty house stood between them and the graveyard. A homemade sign in the front yard of the house said, "For Rent." As the weeks passed, nobody came to look at the house, so my aunt and uncle assumed nobody would be moving in.

Then one day in late October, Aunt Lily noticed that the "For Rent" sign was gone.

"Look, Lawrence," she said. "I think we may be getting new neighbors. I think the house has been rented."

A couple of days later, the new neighbors, the Brays, moved in. There was a man, John; a woman, Mattie; a boy, Ben, who was about thirteen years old; and a girl, Sara, about nine. Aunt Lily and Uncle Lawrence walked over and introduced themselves and asked if there was anything they could do.

"Thanks," John told him, "but I think we are all settled in."

Uncle Lawrence smiled at the kids.

"Do you think you'll be scared living next door to a graveyard on Halloween?" he asked.

John spoke up before they could answer.

"We don't believe in ghosts or celebrating Halloween. It's just foolishness. Living by a graveyard is just like living anywhere else."

"Well, I always heard it was bad luck," said Uncle Lawrence. "I never did like to tempt fate. I hope all goes well. Just let us know if you need anything."

John Bray simply nodded and said nothing else. Uncle Lawrence and Aunt Lily went back to their house and went about their own business.

The new family didn't seem to be inclined to socialize. The Brays nodded and spoke if they and Uncle Lawrence and Aunt Lily happened to be in the yard at the same time, but they never came to visit. My uncle and aunt respected their privacy and did not intrude.

One day, though, Uncle Lawrence happened to be in the backyard at the same time as the Bray boy, Ben.

"Who's buried in that grave off to itself at the back of the graveyard?" Ben asked. "I was over there late yesterday afternoon, but I couldn't find a marker."

"I haven't lived here long, Ben, so I don't know firsthand, but I heard down at the store that the man who is buried there used to live in your house," Uncle Lawrence answered. "His name was Ernest Haskins, I believe they said. My hearing isn't always what it used to be."

"What did he die of?" Ben asked.

"What I heard was that he killed himself," said my uncle. "He couldn't make the payments on his house, so the bank foreclosed and told Ernest he'd have to move. He was very upset and angry. He said that he'd die first, and I suppose he decided right then to shoot himself. In any case, he didn't leave that house under his own power. They had to carry him out and bury him."

"But why did they bury him just outside the graveyard fence, and why didn't they put up a headstone?" Ben wanted to know.

"Church people didn't think it was fitting. They thought it was sinful to bury a corpse on sacred ground with Christian people if the deceased had taken his own life. I don't guess he had any family to put up a proper marker. The whole thing was very sad," said my uncle. "Some people have said to me that they have seen Ernest's ghost around and inside your house at night. I guess that's why it was so hard to rent."

"My dad doesn't care about tales like that," said Ben. "He doesn't believe in ghosts, but Sara and I aren't so sure. Last night we were on the porch and looked across the graveyard. A white mist covered that grave—Ernest's grave—and there wasn't any mist over any other grave. We told our dad, but he said it was just fog and to get on up to bed. I looked out my window, though, and I saw that mist turn into a shape like a man and drift toward the house. Dad yelled again for us to get in bed, so I don't know where the mist went. Later in the night, I woke up and it seemed like there was someone else in the room. I finally went back to sleep."

John came outside as Ben finished his story.

"Ben!" he called. "Don't you have chores to do? You don't have time to stand around talking all day!"

"I'd better go," said Ben. He hurried off to try to catch up with his father.

Uncle Lawrence always liked a spooky story. He looked out the window to see if he could see the mist that night, but he couldn't see the grave from his window.

About a week passed, and a neighbor down the road died from a stroke. They buried him in the graveyard, leaving the fresh dirt covered with flowers.

After everybody had gone, Aunt Lily was out in her backyard taking her wash down from the clothesline when she noticed Mattie Bray headed for the new grave with two flowerpots and a little garden shovel. Aunt Lily watched as

Mattie filled the pots with dirt and came back across to her yard. Then she noticed that Aunt Lily had been watching her.

"I wanted to repot some flowers," Mattie said. "I thought the fresh dirt would be rich and easy to get. The rest of the ground seems so hard now."

"Yes," said Aunt Lily. "I guess it is rich, but I've always heard it's bad luck to take dirt from a graveyard, especially a fresh grave."

Mattie just laughed.

"I don't believe in all that nonsense," she said.

She took her pots and went inside, and Aunt Lily took her clothes and did likewise.

Halloween came and went. Most of the neighbors celebrated with jack-o'-lanterns and treats for the children—all except the Brays. Maybe it was Halloween that set off the events that followed.

On Sunday at church, Mattie stopped to talk to Aunt Lily after they came outside.

"Do you really think it's bad luck to take the dirt from the grave?" she asked Aunt Lily.

"It's what I've always heard," she answered. "Why do you ask?"

"I've seen a shadow around my flowerpots every night," confided Mattie. "John says the shadows are from tree limbs, but there are no limbs outside the kitchen window where I keep my flowers."

"Maybe you should put the dirt back," suggested Aunt Lily.

"I was going to, but John said he'd have no such nonsense," said Mattie. "He can be very stubborn about such things."

"Maybe he'll change his mind," said Aunt Lily. "Sometimes a man has to learn for himself. Maybe things will happen to make him reconsider."

And happen they did! Aunt Lily and Uncle Lawrence only learned of the events later, when the Brays were loading their belongings and moving away.

The first thing was a crash that woke the Brays in the middle of the night. They rushed to their kitchen and saw both flowerpots shattered on the floor. Mattie swept up the dirt and broken pieces of the clay pots and took them back to the graveyard as soon as daylight came. There were no more shadows at the window after that, so Mattie thought that that spirit must now be at rest.

But there were other happenings that indicated an angrier presence had come into the house. Ben saw the mist rise every night from the grave and float toward the house. At first there were knocks, and then loud banging. At other times, they would hear eerie, but indistinct, whispers. At night, the cover would be yanked from the bed where John and Mattie slept, or at least tried to sleep.

The final straw came when Sara's screams filled the house one night. They rushed to her room and found her sobbing. Scratch marks were visible on the side of her face. She hadn't seen what did it, but she had been terrified for her life. As they all stood there not knowing what to do, a loud whisper told them, *Get out of my house!* They followed the suggestion.

A few days after the Brays had moved, Uncle Lawrence decided to walk over to Ernest Haskins's grave. He was shocked to see stakes driven deep into the ground all around the grave. Chains crisscrossing the grave were locked securely to the stakes. He never knew who did it. And he never knew if the chains kept Ernest in the grave. Maybe John installed the stakes and chains before he and his family went away. Or maybe it was someone else who lived nearby.

Uncle Lawrence and Aunt Lily moved away soon after the Brays left. Nobody else moved into the house by the graveyard during the short time they were there.

Of course, there is no proof that it's bad luck to live by a cemetery, but the things that the Brays experienced provide a great deal of evidence to support the belief.

The Octagon House

At the 2014 Southern Festival of Books in Bowling Green, Kentucky, several people stopped by our table and asked if we had heard of Octagon House. Most of them had information or stories to share before they moved on. They pointed out that Octagon House is not far from Bowling Green.

Octagon House (also referred to as Octagon Hall) is located in Simpson County at 6040 Bowling Green Road, just north of Franklin, Kentucky. When Andrew Jackson Caldwell built the house in the mid-1800s, he wanted something unique, so he had eight sides built instead of the usual four.

It is said that during the Civil War, Caldwell offered shelter to many Confederate soldiers. Civil War reenactments are sometimes held there now. Those who participate sometimes experience things they cannot explain, such as footsteps and the opening and closing of doors throughout the night.

The Caldwell family continued to occupy the house even after Andrew's death in 1866. In 1918, his widow, Harriet, sold the house to a Nashville osteopath, Doctor Miles Williams. He lived in the house until his death in 1954.

His heirs turned it into rental property until 2001, when The Octagon Hall Foundation obtained the building and became dedicated to restoring and preserving the house and grounds.

Some people who stopped to tell us stories about the place said that they have experienced strange smells in the parlor where Andrew's body was laid out. They also mention seeing the ghost of a man riding a wagon in the backyard. It is thought to be Andrew Caldwell.

A young Western Kentucky University student told us the most intriguing story of all. In the 1800s, she said, there was a little girl (one website calls her Mary Elizabeth) who was helping prepare a meal for the Caldwells in the basement, a place called the Winter Kitchen. She got too close to the fireplace, caught fire, and burned to death.

On some tours, visitors hear the girl's footsteps beside them, and some say she has held their hand. Others say they have had a fleeting glance of a figure in the Winter Kitchen. The figure seems to appear and vanish quickly.

During one of the Halloween tours at the Octagon

House in 2003, the fireplace kettle on a movable arm mysteriously swung out into the room. The student assured us that this was not part of the tour. Perhaps the little ghost is lonely and wants attention.

To check out this site for yourselves, go to the Octagon Hall Museum website and make a reservation. They allow legitimate ghost-hunting groups to book investigations, but they discourage those who simply consider it a lark to spend a night in a haunted house.

If you are looking for a "fake" Halloween haunted house where you can giggle and scream, the Octagon House is not for you. If you are looking for a Halloween treat and have respect for the dead, this is the perfect place to go.

Veterans Day

We will start our chapter on Veterans Day with a grammatical note about the title. There is some difference in spelling on calendars and elsewhere. Some sources spell it "Veteran's Day"; others, "Veterans' Day." The United States government has declared that the official rendering is the simple plural, with no apostrophe.

Veterans Day is celebrated on November 11. Originally called Armistice Day to honor the end of World War I, the name was changed to Veterans Day by Congress on June 1, 1954, to honor all those who served in the U.S. armed forces.

On Veterans Day, nonessential government offices are closed, all federal workers are paid for the holiday, and no mail is delivered.

Some restaurants offer free meals to veterans on that day.

On this day, the president of the United States places a wreath on the Tomb of the Unknowns at Arlington National Cemetery, and veterans' organizations hold parades.

Veterans Day is a time for all of us to pause, remember,

and express our thanks to those who fought that we might be free.

A Veterans Day Civil War Tale

We have veterans on both sides of our families, and our families hold these veterans in the highest regard. We honor, respect, and love them, and we remember them in our stories on Veterans Day.

Lonnie has a story about his family and the Civil War, and he tells it this way.

Two young men on my side of the family, Elijah and Malachi Brown, are subjects of one of my favorite Civil War stories. They were brothers, about a year apart in age.

Elijah and Malachi were sons of Jonathan and Sara Ann Brown, and they lived and worked on the family farm in Wayne County. The family supported the Confederacy, but the boys delayed joining up because they were needed to do farm work.

On long summer nights, the family gathered round on the porch and listened to Jonathan or Elijah play the fiddle. Malachi and Sara joined in by clapping their hands and sometimes singing. It was the best relief they had from the stress of war all around them.

Times were extremely hard. When reports came that the Yanks were approaching, families, including the Browns, would hide all their valuables—food, silverware, and jewelry—in caves or bury them so the enemy would not take them.

The families themselves would sometimes hide in caves, taking with them their children and pets. If the pets were loud enough to attract attention and became a threat to the family, the family would kill the animals so they would not lead the enemy to the cave where they were hiding.

The Brown boys wanted to take care of their family, but they longed to fight for what they believed in, too. The year finally came when they knew they had to join the action. That year, they tended the crops, harvested them, and stored them in the safest places they could find on the farm. They wanted the harvest to be safe for the family in case the Yanks came through.

It was the end of October when all was finished. The young men sat down with their parents and told them they would be leaving the next morning.

Sara Ann's eyes filled with tears, but she understood that this was something they had to do.

"I'll pack some food for you in the morning," she said.

"I want you to take the fiddle," said Jonathan. "It will keep you company when you miss your home."

The boys nodded in agreement.

The next morning, Elijah and Malachi said good-bye to their parents. They took the food and the fiddle and started over the hills to become Confederate soldiers. That was the last time their parents saw them alive.

When the family had heard no word from their sons, Jonathan walked over the hills to the town where they had headed to sign up. It was November 11, long before Veterans

Day was named a holiday, but it was a day burned in Jonathan's mind forever after. The records showed that his boys had signed up, but nobody had seen them since.

That night, Sara Ann and Jonathan heard music. It was warm for early November, and they were sitting on the porch, waiting for the house to cool down after the heat from cooking supper.

"That sounds like Elijah playing the fiddle!" said Sara Ann.

"It certainly does sound like him," said Jonathan. "His style is unique."

"Maybe their regiment is camped nearby! Maybe they will pass by here and stop tomorrow. I'd love to see them!" said Sara Ann.

"I would, too," said Jonathan. "I'd like to see how they're doing."

The old couple went to bed with high expectations that night. Maybe they would get to see their sons one more time before they went into battle.

Morning came, but the two young men didn't come. Sara Ann and Jonathan waited until midafternoon before they gave up watching.

Jonathan decided to climb up the hill where he'd heard the music playing the night before to see if he could see a sign of a campsite. When he got there, though, he could find no evidence that anyone had camped there.

Puzzled, Jonathan enlisted the help of his neighbors. They searched the hill, but found nothing.

That winter was harsh, but Sara Ann and Jonathan survived on the food their sons had left for them. When Jonathan was in town and met any rebel soldiers passing through, he asked if they had met Elijah or Malachi, but the answer was always no.

Night after night, even when they were inside the house, Sara Ann and Jonathan heard the fiddle playing in the distance. It moved around sometimes, and they couldn't figure out the source. Sara Ann began to think that they were the only ones hearing it, but she asked the neighbors about it and they confirmed that they were hearing it, too.

Then, the music stopped. It was a year before they heard it again. They heard it every year after that at the same time the boys disappeared.

Except for the fiddle music, they never had any other contact from their sons. The mystery of their disappearance was never solved.

I have heard tales, though, about people still hearing fiddle music as they come across that hill in Wayne County. Maybe the two young men are still there, playing the fiddle and thinking of home.

Our family will always think of Elijah and Malachi Brown and wonder what happened to the two brave young men who went off to be soldiers.

Thanksgiving Day

In America, we celebrate Thanksgiving on the fourth Thursday in November. According to history, the Pilgrims held a three-day feast to celebrate a bountiful harvest in the fall of 1621. Many consider this the first Thanksgiving.

Thanksgiving became an official holiday in 1863 with a proclamation by President Abraham Lincoln during the Civil War.

Today our national traditional Thanksgiving feast normally includes roast turkey with stuffing, cranberry sauce, mashed potatoes with gravy or sweet potatoes, sweet corn, green beans or green peas, corn bread, biscuits, and pumpkin or mince pie.

Besides the feasting, there are other ways to celebrate. Football is an important part of many Thanksgiving celebrations. Where we grew up, "turkey trots" were held—races consisting of a five-mile run and a two-mile walk, with a turkey as the prize for the winner. In New York City, Macy's Thanksgiving Day Parade has been held each year since 1924. The parade features floats, balloons, and marching bands.

Santa's float ends the parade, indicating the beginning of the Christmas season.

Thanksgiving is a spiritual time and a family time, and it often draws ghosts, too.

Lucian's Mystery Chaser

When Lonnie's father, Lucian Brown, was a very young man, he, like most all other young men in the Gentry's Mill area, liked to hunt. He took great pride in his rifle and tried to take good care of it. As Thanksgiving approached, he cleaned it and prepared to shoot a turkey for Thanksgiving dinner.

The day before Thanksgiving, Lucian took his rifle out early in the morning and went off to find a wild turkey. It seemed as though the turkeys knew he was coming, though, and kept themselves out of sight. Eventually, he had to give up the hunt and go home to help his dad work.

At quitting time, Lucian took his rifle and hurried into the woods again to see if the turkeys had come out of hiding.

"Don't be too long," his mother called. "I've got supper on cooking!"

"Okay," he called back to her, even though supper was not the first thing on his mind right now. He was determined to get a turkey!

He kept going deep into the woods, but he saw no signs of a turkey. He was very disappointed because he would have felt very good to have provided the turkey for the family meal.

The woods began to get dark, and Lucian heard thunder fairly close. It didn't storm that often in autumn, but he didn't want to be in the woods even if it just rained with no thunder and lightning. He knew that it soon would be hard to see, so he thought that maybe he should head on home.

As he was deciding what to do, he heard a noise in the leaves behind him. It was hard to see anything among the trees, and he became uneasy. He had heard a report of a possible bear sighting a few days earlier, and he wanted to take no chances.

He started to walk quickly toward home, but he heard an odd sound behind him. Was it a growl or a cough? He looked back, but there was nothing visible. He heard the sound again, and he began to run. He stubbed his toe on a log beside the path and lost his balance. His rifle went flying out of his hand and landed in the leaves. Something was crashing toward him now, so, not waiting to get the rifle, Lucian ran for his life.

He had gone farther into the woods than he thought, so he was beginning to get breathless running to get out. He dared not stop, though, because something was following him for sure. It sounded like something on two feet, and it seemed to be gaining on him. The storm was right overhead now, and the cloud was dark and menacing.

He ran and ran, his heart thumping loudly all the way. Finally, he saw the light in his house just beyond the edge of the woods. With one last burst of speed, he nearly knocked down the door and fell inside, just as the storm broke.

The family gathered around, concerned about his heavy breathing.

"What happened?" his dad asked.

"Something was chasing me in the woods!" Lucian gasped. "It came right up to the edge of the tree line."

His brothers ran and looked out, but with the wind and rain, they couldn't see anything.

"I tell you, something was chasing me!" declared Lucian.

"It was just your imagination," his mom said. "You were hearing your own heartbeat."

Everybody laughed except Lucian and his father.

"Where's your rifle?" his father asked sternly.

"I dropped it in the woods," Lucian replied.

"So that's the way you take care of your gun?" his dad continued.

"You're right," he told his dad. "I'm sorry. I'll go back now and get it."

"Not in this storm, you won't, young man," said his mother. "The damage is already done anyway."

"But I wanted us to have a turkey for Thanksgiving, Mom," he told her. "It's just not Thanksgiving without a turkey!"

"We will have one," she smiled. "Your father and brothers went hunting, too, and they got a nice big one."

Lucian felt terrible. He had run away and left his rifle, which by now was surely all wet and muddy. It was probably just his imagination anyway. Nothing had likely been chasing him at all.

He fell asleep, thinking that he would go get his rifle in the morning, even before he ate his breakfast.

Everybody was already up when he woke up the next morning, waiting for breakfast. Nobody had been outside.

Lucian went to the door and opened it to see if the rain had finally stopped. He gasped in surprise.

"Come look at this," he said.

The family rushed to the door and stared at the place he was pointing. There on the porch, safe and dry, was his rifle, leaning against the wall by the door.

Lonnie's father never solved the mystery. Had a local hunter followed him, trying to give him the rifle? If so, why didn't he knock on the door and give it to him? Or had some spirit hunter brought the rifle because he remembered how important his rifle had been to him when he was alive?

Whatever had happened to bring the rifle home remained a mystery, but Lonnie's dad had a thankful heart when he sat down that day with his family for Thanksgiving dinner.

The Corpse Candle

Roberta's grandmother, Fanny Dean, passed along many stories of the supernatural through Roberta's mother, Lillian Dean Simpson. Roberta was always fascinated by corpse candles after she heard this story.

A corpse candle is a little light carried by a ghost. The flickering of the light looks like the flickering of a real candle. It got the name of corpse candle because it is carried by a ghost and is usually seen just prior to someone's death.

Grandma Fanny had heard of corpse candles and sometimes thought she saw them bobbing along near the church graveyard by Damron's Creek when she was a child. It was not in her nature to check out mysterious lights at night, so she never went outside to look up close. Those flickering lights scared her a little.

When they were first married, Grandma Fanny and Grandpa Mike lived on a farm near Damron's Creek. Their closest neighbors were a couple and their grown son, who lived up the creek about half a mile. Mr. and Mrs. Byrne and their son, Toby, kept to themselves mostly, but were always pleasant when Grandma and Grandpa met them at church or the store.

One Sunday, the Byrnes did not show up at church. Later that day, Toby passed the Deans' house, headed for the doctor. Grandma Fanny decided to walk up the creek to see if she could help. Even before the doctor arrived, Grandma Fanny could tell that Mrs. Byrne was in a bad way.

The doctor diagnosed it as the flu. In the few days that followed, Grandma Fanny went up every day and helped out all she could. Mrs. Byrne grew weaker and weaker, though, and died with her husband and son by her side.

Life was very hard for Mr. Byrne and Toby without her. Mrs. Byrne had always done a large share of the work on the farm, and the two men had to take on her duties as well as their own.

One day, Grandma Fanny ran into Toby at the store. She asked Toby how he and his father were doing.

"I'm fine, but Dad is overworking. I can't get him to slow down or go see the doctor," Toby answered. "I have offered to get a job in town to make more money and make things easier, but he says no."

"Mike works too hard, too," she said. "I can't get him to slow down either. There is always something to do on the farm."

Grandma Fanny gave the two Byrne men no more thought until she heard at church later that Toby had indeed carried out his plan. He had gone into town and taken a job at the nearby sawmill. It was about two weeks after that when Toby came by and told her about his encounter with the corpse candle.

There was no phone on the farm, so Toby couldn't call during the week while he was at work at the sawmill. He planned to go home every weekend and help his dad with the farm work, so he really didn't need to call home during the week. Late that November the weekend would be extended because Thanksgiving meant that the mill would be closed Thursday through Sunday.

Toby had taken a room at a boardinghouse near his work. After supper, he liked to sit on the front porch until bedtime, like he had done back home. It was a warm November, and the night air was just right.

He had worked hard that Tuesday and was particularly happy to relax in the porch swing and enjoy the peaceful night sounds. Suddenly, everything got quiet. No crickets! No fall bugs! Nothing was rustling in the leaves.

Then he saw something coming down the road carrying a candle. The light was flickering as it bobbed up and down. He couldn't see who was carrying the light, but he could make out an indistinct figure. It came to the end of the walk and stopped. Then it stepped back a few steps and came to the end of the walk again. It repeated this process three times.

I think it wants me to follow it, Toby thought.

He had an uneasy feeling that grew stronger as he explained to his landlady that he needed to borrow a horse to go home.

"At this time of night?" she asked, very surprised. "What on earth for?"

"I can't explain it," he told her. "There is a light outside that seems to want me to follow it. I am afraid something's wrong at home."

"A light?" she said, looking out the window. "Oh, you must go!" she said to him. "That's a corpse candle! Somebody is going to die."

He saddled the borrowed horse and soon was on his way. The light flickered along in front of him. A few hours later, when he came in sight of his house, the corpse candle went out. There was a light in his father's window, though, and Toby knew his dad would never be up at that hour unless he was ill.

Toby tied up the horse and ran inside. He heard his father call out from his bedroom. Toby found him there on the floor. He had become dizzy and had fallen, breaking his leg. He had struggled, but could not get up alone.

"Thank God you came," said his dad. "How did you know?"

Toby told him about the corpse candle.

Toby helped his father to the doctor. The leg was set and Mr. Byrne was able to spend Thanksgiving at home.

Toby returned the horse, picked up all the fixings for a Thanksgiving Day dinner, and prepared a feast for him and his father.

That night they sat on the front porch until the night air became too chilly for Mr. Byrne. As they got up to go inside, a light danced across the drive and disappeared.

"I remember wishing your mother and you were here," said his dad.

Toby nodded.

"That was your mother for sure," said his dad. "She came for you because she knew how guilty you would feel if anything happened to me when you were not here to help me. I might have died if you hadn't come."

"Yes," said Toby. "You certainly might have."

"That light at the drive just now was your mother, too," said Mr. Byrne. "She's happy everything worked out all right."

Toby agreed. He went back to the sawmill and got his last paycheck. He got the few belongings he had left at the boardinghouse and came back home to stay.

Grandma Dean remembered how she had feared corpse candles all her life, but after a corpse candle saved Mr. Byrne, she wasn't afraid of them much anymore.

Grandma's Pumpkin Pie

Roberta's Grandma Simpson said that her Grandmother Alley made the best pumpkin pies she ever ate. Each year the entire family looked forward to Thanksgiving because Grandma Alley made plenty of pumpkin pies for everybody. She let Grandma Simpson help her so she could watch and learn. Grandma Simpson got pretty good at making pies like Grandma Alley.

The year Grandma Alley died was a sad one indeed. She died in late summer, but everybody was already thinking about Thanksgiving. How could they celebrate without her pumpkin pies?

Then another event occurred that seemed to make the pumpkin pie possibility more unlikely.

The Carter family, who lived across the creek, had a young male relative, Hollis, who was visiting from Ohio. Hollis was bored and hated having to stay in the country for the duration of the visit. He knew nothing about farming and only wanted to go back to city life.

Mr. Carter did not raise watermelons and pumpkins on his farm.

"Nobody in the family likes pumpkins and watermelons," he said, "so why should I waste my space, time, and energy to grow the things? I can think of better things to plant in my fields."

He was wrong about one family member. Hollis loved watermelon!

One night, after everybody had gone to bed early, Hollis was restless and couldn't sleep.

Maybe I could sleep if I had a watermelon, he thought. *It would be so cool! Now, I wonder who grows some around here. Oh, yeah. The Alleys.*

Hollis walked across the yard, picked up a stick to use as a walking stick, and headed to the Alleys' farm. Everybody was in bed there, too, so he didn't worry about being caught. He found a watermelon, broke it open with his stick, and enjoyed the cool, juicy contents. As he finished off the last bite, he heard a voice behind him.

"You didn't have to steal a watermelon," said Mr. Alley, holding his rifle. "I would have given you one if you had asked."

Mr. Alley felt that Hollis's family should know what he had done, so he marched Hollis home and told the family what had happened. Mr. Alley didn't ask them to punish Hollis. He just thought they should know about the stealing so it wouldn't become a problem.

Mr. Carter did punish Hollis, though. After Mr. Alley left, Mr. Carter broke a switch from the peach tree and took Hollis out behind the woodshed and gave him a good thrashing with the switch. Hollis wasn't hurt, but he was angry.

The next night, he waited even later, until he was sure

everybody was asleep. Then he picked up a stronger stick with a keen point at the edge of the yard and walked straight to the fields at the Alley place. He walked through the large pumpkin and watermelon patch and smashed every watermelon and pumpkin in the patch. All were ruined!

That ended Hollis's visit. Mr. Carter shipped the young man back home to let his parents deal with him. The parents paid Mr. Alley for the damage, but some of the damage was beyond price. With all the pumpkins ruined, there would be no pumpkin pies.

Grandma Simpson was heartbroken. She had Grandma Alley's recipe, but not the principal ingredient. On Thanksgiving eve, the family went to bed feeling very sad.

The next morning, in the wee hours of Thanksgiving Day, Grandma Simpson put the turkey in the oven to roast. She heard a noise that she couldn't identify on the front porch. She opened the door and looked out, but nobody was there.

She spotted something on the edge of the porch and moved closer. There were two of the biggest, healthiest pumpkins she had ever seen! The neighbors could not have brought them because they didn't grow them. Who could have done such a kind deed?

Grandma Simpson picked them up and took them inside to make the pumpkin pies. She swore until the end of her life that, as she picked up the pumpkins, she heard Grandma Alley laughing!

Pearl Harbor Day

Americans remember Pearl Harbor Day each year on December 7. The surprise attack by the Japanese forces on that date in 1941 on Pearl Harbor, Hawaii, killed more than 2,400 military personnel and drew the United States into World War II.

President Franklin D. Roosevelt called it "a day which will live in infamy" and declared that no matter how long it might take to overcome the invasion, the American people would win through to absolute victory. The day after the attack, the United States declared war on Japan.

Pearl Harbor was a strategic military base in the Pacific. The U.S. Naval headquarters was there. The United States strictly enforced economic embargos, and Japan, trying to expand, suffered because of this. Nobody dreamed that the Japanese would dare attack the U.S. Navy. In the months that followed the Japanese attack, the slogan "Remember Pearl Harbor" swept the country.

Today, people across America hold ceremonies and give speeches to remember the sacrifice of those who died in the

Pearl Harbor attack. On Pearl Harbor Day, dignitaries often honor the dead by placing flowers or leis in the water.

In 1994, Congress designated December 7 a day of national observance to honor those who died or were injured in the Japanese attack.

Pearl Harbor Soldier

Roberta was born in 1939 and Lonnie was born in 1937. As children we heard talk about the war every day, but we were too young to understand completely what was going on. We only understood that family members and friends were going away to fight in that war.

Roberta tells this story about something that happened to her sister during the war.

When my sister Fatima was in her teens, she considered it a very pleasant duty to write to the soldiers she knew. Harsh censorship was applied to letters in those days. I can still remember how Fatima's letters from the soldiers were sometimes cut into shreds because the government took out anything that might indicate where the location of the soldier might be.

One of our neighbors, Ray, who had volunteered for the army, was stationed in Pearl Harbor. Fatima wrote to him every week. Ray was very happy that he might soon get shipped back to the States.

December was approaching, and Ray's family was very excited, hoping that he might be home for the holidays.

Every night, most families in our community gathered around their battery radios to hear news of the war that was being fought in Europe. My family did the same.

December came, and Fatima and I started the Christmas countdown.

"I bet if Ray gets home for Christmas, his mom and dad will give him a party!" said Fatima. "I know we'll get to go!"

I knew she was right. When a soldier came home from wherever he was stationed, even if it was only for a furlough, the whole neighborhood rejoiced and wanted to see him.

Fatima and I went to bed early the night of December 6. The next morning, Fatima got up and was overjoyed.

"Ray's home!" she told us. "I woke up and looked out the window last night. I saw him walking down the road on his way home!"

"He must be tired if he got in late," said my mom. "He'll probably sleep late and come over to say hello after he's had a good breakfast."

Then Dad turned the radio on. The news was tragic—unbelievable! We, along with the rest of the world, were shocked to hear about the sneak attack on Pearl Harbor by the Japanese.

"Looks like Ray got out just in time," my dad commented.

The day went on, but Ray did not come to see us. Finally, Mom walked over to see Ray's family and ask about Ray. She came home to tell us that Ray had not come home at all.

"But I saw him," Fatima insisted. "I would know Ray anywhere."

We didn't know what to think. We thought Fatima must have been dreaming, although she was sure she wasn't.

Finally, the waiting ended. Ray's father came to tell us the news. The family had received a telegram saying that Ray was among the casualties at Pearl Harbor.

What had Fatima seen? Was it a neighbor that she thought was Ray? She was sure it wasn't. It was her belief that Ray's ghost had come back to walk down the road home one last time.

Hanukkah

There were no Jewish residents in Roberta's neighborhood when she was growing up. She learned about the Jews from her Bible studies in Sunday school. Even though she did not understand their rich traditions, she was always eager to learn about people with different beliefs than her own.

Hanukkah is a Jewish holiday celebrated for eight days and nights sometime between late November and late December on the secular calendar. In Hebrew, the word "Hanukkah" means "dedication." This holiday commemorates the rededication of the holy Temple in Jerusalem following the Jewish victory over the Syrian-Greeks. By the time the Jews returned to the temple, it had been spiritually defiled by the worship of foreign gods and the sacrificing of swine.

The victorious Jews were determined to purify the Temple of Jerusalem by burning ritual oil in the temple's menorah (candelabrum) for eight days. They were dismayed to find they had only enough oil for one day. They lit the menorah anyway, and the small amount of oil lasted for the full eight days! This is the miracle celebrated every year when Jews light the candles of the menorah at Hanukkah.

Go to the Light

Roberta especially liked one story told to her by her Grandmother Simpson. She had heard it from her sister, Barbara Jane, who learned the story while visiting relatives in south central Kentucky.

The story goes this way.

A Jewish lady, one of the few Jewish people who lived in that neighborhood, said that the reason for the Hanukkah lights was not to illuminate the inside of the house, but rather to have the lights show outside, so that anyone going by the house could see the light and be reminded of the miracle of the holiday.

That was an important concept in this story.

In 1939, a Jewish man left Poland with his eldest daughter and her husband. They could speak a little English, so they planned to find work in the United States and earn enough to bring over the old man's wife and son.

They arrived in New York on August 23. One week later, Poland fell to the Germans, and the man's wife, son, and everybody else they left behind were lost to them forever.

America had been a land of promise, but the old man and his daughter and son-in-law were unable to get work in New York. The family moved to Kentucky and managed to claim a small farm. They worked hard and eked out a living.

Every year, they celebrated Hanukkah proudly because they did not have to do so in secret in their new country.

As the years passed, the old man became ill and frail. He spent most of the time in his bedroom on the second floor in the front of the house. His daughter moved the menorah to her father's room, so he could light the candles in the window. He firmly believed in the miracle of the light.

The light was shown for those passing by through all those years.

At last the old man died, and his daughter and son-in-law sold the farm and moved away. The new owner did not want to live in the old house, so he tore it down and built a one-story house in the same location.

Life went on, and eventually people forgot about the old man who lit the Hanukkah candles every year.

One year, winter came early, and it was a hard one. The new owner was coming home from town one night when a regular snowstorm turned into a blizzard.

He wasn't too far from home, but the visibility was only about two feet, so he knew he could wander in circles and freeze to death. He did not know it was Hanukkah, but he stopped, closed his eyes, and prayed for a miracle.

When he opened his eyes, the snow had lessened. He could see lights flickering through the snow, and he walked toward them. They led him to his own home. Something just kept telling him in his mind to go to the light.

"It was strange," he said later. "The lights were just above my house, like there was a second floor. They kept shining until I was safely inside, just like the miracle I needed. It was like they burned just long enough to fill my need and then they were gone."

Had he seen through a time warp into the past when the old man lit the candles in his second-floor room to spread the light on Hanukkah?

Christmas

Christmas Day is a Christian holiday marking the birth of Jesus Christ. It is celebrated on December 25. In 1893 all the states of the United States declared Christmas a federal holiday, and it has been our biggest holiday ever since.

At Christmastime, most homes and businesses are decorated with sparkling lights, Christmas trees, and symbols of legends such as snowmen, Santa Claus, reindeer, candy canes, holly, mistletoe, and religious nativity scenes.

People sing carols, read, attend concerts and plays, go for sleigh rides, and eat treats of candy, cakes, and pies. Many children hang stockings for Santa to fill on Christmas Eve, when he is said to come down the chimney.

One of the most popular activities is to carry on the tradition of telling ghost stories. These are some we would love to share with you.

Jingle Bells

Roberta tells this story of one Christmas, when she was seven years old.

According to custom, our neighbors came to visit on Christmas night to stay until bedtime and tell stories. I can't remember all the stories told that night, but I remember the one our neighbor Mrs. Anna told. She and her family lived on the farm that joined Grandmother Simpson's place.

"The snow from Christmas Eve still lay on the ground, settled in to stay with no intention of melting," she began.

"It's laying on for another one," my mother said as always.

We all nodded in agreement. Most of the neighbors had heard her say that, and usually she was right.

"I wasn't thinking about the snow," continued Mrs. Anna. "I was holding tightly to my new doll that Santa had brought me and I was listening to the stories.

"I once lived by a neighbor who had mental problems," said Mrs. Anna. "The girl, Mindy, was kept at home because there were no facilities for the mentally impaired in those days. Some people locked the mentally disturbed persons in the attic or chained them in the basement. Lots of horror stories came from those conditions.

"Mindy's disposition was not dangerous, so her family let her roam freely inside the house. They kept the doors locked, but she became very skilled at getting out anyway, through an open window or a door the family had unintentionally left open. When Mindy got out, she would roam the neighborhood.

"Nobody was afraid of her, but when she showed up at neighbors' houses, they knew her family would miss her and be worried, so, unless a storm was coming, they would send her on her way.

"'Go on home now, Mindy,' they would tell her. 'Your mom will be looking for you.'

"I always liked Mindy, though, so I would often ask her to stay and play for a while. Mindy liked it when we made mud pies and pretended to cook them.

"Some people were amazed at how Mindy could always find her way home. It was odd since she was limited in other things. Of course, she took her own time about going. She liked to be outside in all kinds of weather.

"Her mother sometimes wanted her home immediately and would go out looking for her. It was hard to find her until her mom got the idea of making her daughter a jingle-bell necklace. Mindy wore it every day, all year round. When her mom wanted to find her in a hurry, she would go outside and listen for the jingle bells.

"One day in winter, the weather turned foul, giving the countryside an eerie look. The snow covered the hills and the fields and the farmhouses like white sheets covering the dead. Mindy's mom told Mindy not to go out that day and locked the doors to make sure Mindy stayed inside. Then she began to prepare supper while Mindy played in her bedroom.

"Mindy's mother decided she would make a peach cobbler for supper, so she dashed out to the cellar to get a jar of the peaches she had canned. Back inside, she put the jar down and closed the door, but she forgot to lock it. While she was cooking and humming to herself, Mindy moved silently by her and disappeared like a ghost into the snow.

"Mindy saw a bunny hopping in the snow, so she followed it down the slope into the pasture. The slope was slick, and Mindy slipped and rolled down the slope to the field. Her jingle-bell necklace broke and fell off her neck.

"Mindy tried to get up, but her ankle hurt. She could only lie there wondering where the rabbit had gone.

"Mindy was tired, and she felt very sleepy. Slowly, her eyes closed and she fell forward on the ground fast asleep.

"When her mother missed her, she began to look for her. The jingle-bell necklace was silent, and Mindy's tracks were almost covered. Mindy's mother had to proceed slowly through the snow, but she managed to follow the tracks to the place where Mindy lay.

"Struggling, she carried Mindy home and tried to revive her. It was too late, though. Mindy had gone to sleep for the last time.

"After her death, people missed her, but after a while they said that on snowy nights they could hear jingle bells out in the snow. Some swore they met the ghost of Mindy on her way home on cold winter nights.

"I never really believed people who said that, but I found out one Christmas night that it was true.

"The threat of snow was in the air. We were all at home enjoying our Christmas Day, when my little brother Jimmy said he didn't feel too well. He didn't eat anything at supper. Even his favorite Christmas goodies didn't tempt him. He felt hot to touch.

"Mom put him to bed and went to her herb cabinet to get some herbs to brew into a tea to break the fever. 'Oh, no!' she said. 'I've used up all my herbs. Anna, you'll have to run over to Miss Harmon's house to get some.'

"I loved my little brother and I wanted to help him, but it was almost dark, and Miss Harmon's house was on the other side of the woods. I knew I had no choice, though. Mom had said go, so I had to do it. It was a common practice to send children out day or night to get something that was needed from the country store or a neighbor.

"I put on my boots, coat, scarf, and mittens and started on my way.

"The sky was looking heavy and foreboding as I headed down the road. The first large flakes fell before I reached the woods. It was easy to follow the path, though, because the trees were blocking out part of the snow.

"I was happy to see the light in Miss Harmon's window. She had hot chocolate made, and she insisted that I drink a cup while she packaged the herbs my mother would need. She offered to go home with me, but I told her I would be all right.

"The truth was that I wasn't all right. I knew I was in trouble as soon as I crossed her yard and entered the woods. It was dark now. The trees had been unable to hold back the snow for long, so the path was covered. I should have gone back to Miss Harmon and asked for help, but all I could think about was getting home and getting the herbs for Mom to fix Jimmy's tea. I trudged ahead, not really knowing where I was going.

"Everything looked strange after a while. I began to feel tired and thought I would sit down and rest for a minute on a snow-covered log. I brushed off the snow and sat down. In just a minute, I would go on.

"I began to feel very sleepy. Mom had told me never to go to sleep in the snow or I could freeze to death, but surely it wouldn't hurt to close my eyes for just a minute. My head started to nod, and that's when I heard the jingle bells. They were loud enough to jar me awake.

"*Mindy's jingle bells,* I thought. *She's come to guide me home.*

"At that moment, I had no doubt that she was there. I got to my feet and started to walk, clutching my package of herbs tightly in my hand. My feet and hands were beginning to tingle, but I felt better as I followed the happy sound of the bells. Soon the trees were not so close together, and I could see a light in the window at home.

"'I didn't realize the storm was so close,' my mother said to me. 'I'm sorry I sent you out alone.'

"Mom took the package of herbs and soon had a hot tea brewed for my brother. By bedtime, his fever had broken and he was feeling much better.

"When we had all settled around the fire, I told about following the bells. I thought my family might laugh at me.

"My mother smiled. 'You and Mindy were special friends. I think she led you home because she didn't want you to freeze to death like she did.'

"After we had all gone to bed that night, I lay awake thinking about Mindy. The wind was still howling and swirling the snow around.

"I said a silent thank-you to Mindy for saving my life and for being my friend. Over the wind, I heard the jingle of bells.

"Times have changed, and some of the changes are for the better. It is good now that we have facilities for the mentally impaired. It is good that we no longer have to send children out in the night to do an errand.

"I miss the old times, though, when even death could not come between friends. I listen when I am back home on winter nights and hope that one night I'll hear the jingle of Mindy's bells again as she goes home."

The Christmas Pie

It began as a happy day before Christmas Eve. Kate Atkinson had no way of knowing how sadly it would end.

Kate's parents, younger brother, and grandmother were coming to Kate's house today, the day before Christmas Eve, to stay for a whole week. This was a time before most people owned fast cars that could whiz in with guests, sit parked to allow them to have Christmas dinner, and then drive them away again the same day.

Kate's family was taking the bus from northern Kentucky to Somerset, and then catching a ride on the mail truck from there to the small town that was a little over a mile from the Atkinsons' farm. Kate's husband, Ralph, would take the wagon into town to meet them. Because travel was not easy back then, guests tried to stay a while to make the most of a visit.

Kate had worked hard for days for her family's visit. She'd scrubbed the house, changed the beds, and put her new handmade quilts on the beds instead of the usual bedspreads. She had cleared a place in the parlor for the Christmas tree that Ralph and their son, Richard, always cut fresh and brought to the house on Christmas Eve. Ralph and Richard had stacked plenty of wood on the porch and inside by the fireplace.

Kate had the materials ready for the tree decorations. Everybody would want to help with trimming the tree on Christmas Eve. She had multicolored construction paper and glue to make paper chains and ornaments. Kate was afraid of fire and never allowed the use of candles on the tree. She had gathered holly berries and placed them in a bowl to be strung together and used as chains. There would also be popcorn to make into balls, and bits of cotton to use for snow. Richard had saved chewing gum wrappers since the last Christmas so he could cut the foil into strips for icicles. After the trimming of the tree was finished, Kate knew they would all sit around the fire and sing Christmas carols and tell stories.

She had been able to make some of the food in advance. They would have a turkey for Christmas dinner along with her canned vegetables and the special cake she had made for dessert, but she had a ham baking in the oven for tonight.

She had just finished that night's dessert, two egg custard pies—Ralph's and Richard's favorite—and she had set them on the table to cool just as Ralph came inside and announced it was time for him and Richard to go meet the mail truck.

Richard spied the pies and his eyes lit up.

"Mom," he asked, "could I have a piece of pie before we go?"

"Absolutely not," she replied. "Those are for supper."

"Oh, Mom," he answered.

"My family will be hungry when they get here," Kate said, "so we will eat an early supper. You won't starve 'til then."

"Gee, Mom," Richard persisted. "I'm hungry now. Can't I have just a little piece?"

"No," Kate told him. "Now get on to town and pick up the folks. We wouldn't want them to have to wait in the cold."

"Okay," Richard agreed, and he took one last look at the pies before he and his dad climbed in the wagon and headed to town.

While they were gone, Kate finished preparing the evening meal and left everything, except the pies, on the woodstove to keep warm. She wrapped a couple of last-minute gifts, and finally heard the wagon coming.

The reunion was a joyous one. It had been almost a year since Kate had seen her family, and there were lots of hugs and chatter.

"Mom," said Richard, "are we going to eat soon? I want a slice of pie."

Everybody laughed.

"Okay!" said Kate. "You win!"

Nodding at Richard and her little brother, she said, "Why don't you boys go to the barn and take a look at our new calf while we put the food out?"

The boys dashed off to the barn, and Kate and her mother and grandmother set out the food. Kate was starting to call the boys in to eat when her brother ran to the door, screaming.

"Come quick! Richard was getting some hay from the loft and the ladder slipped and fell on him. He's not moving!"

Ralph, Kate, and the others were out the door, running to the barn as fast as they could move. Richard was on the barn floor with the ladder across his head. A tiny trickle of blood ran from his ear down the side of his neck. Ralph reached him first and checked for a pulse. There was none. He was gone.

Kate remembered hearing her own screams before she fainted. When she woke up, Doc Carter was standing beside the bed. Others were quietly sitting or standing about the room. Suddenly, it came back to her. She threw back the covers and wobbled to the table.

"The pie!" she sobbed. "I've got to give him some pie. He's hungry!"

Ralph put his arm around her.

"Come back to bed," he told her. "He's not hungry now."

The food was untouched on the table, but it was the pies that Kate focused on. This couldn't be happening! Surely Richard would come walking in and they would all sit down to their meal.

"I must insist that you come back to bed," the doctor said. "You have to rest now. You have had a terrible shock."

Kate suddenly snatched up the pies and flung them against the wall. Then she fainted again.

Days passed. Kate was vaguely aware of the funeral. She sat numb and unfeeling most of the time.

Her family stayed a week as they had planned, but not to celebrate the holidays. They stayed to help Ralph and Kate get through the grief, but the sadness prevailed, and eventually they had to go home.

Slowly, life had to be lived again. Kate never forgave herself for refusing to give her son just one piece of pie.

"Why?" she would say. "It was such a small thing that he asked me to do."

She only made one other egg custard pie. She set it out to cool, and a sudden chill filled the kitchen. She felt the presence of someone in the room with her. She looked at the end of the table, and there she saw Richard, standing and smiling at her. When she took a step toward him, he vanished.

Maybe Richard had come to say it was all right. Or maybe he was reminding his mother that she had denied his last request. In any case, it was too much for Kate to bear. She never made another egg custard pie, and even though it was Ralph's favorite, he didn't want her to.

The Christmas Puppy

According to those who knew him, Roberta's grandfather, Louis Franklin Simpson, was a much-admired storyteller and entertainer. Traveling was in his blood, so he didn't spend a lot of time on the farm. He liked to join the turkey drives and provide the drovers with entertainment in the form of songs, dances, and stories.

Turkey drives in Kentucky were akin to cattle drives in the west.

Drovers would herd turkeys in droves to market. It was a known fact, however, that the turkeys were in charge. If something spooked them or if they got tired, they took to the trees to roost. The drovers had no choice but to camp for the night at the location selected by the turkeys. Since these sites were sometimes quite isolated, the men especially enjoyed the talents of Grandpa Louis. He was their only distraction on these lonely nights.

Grandpa Louis died before Roberta was born, so she never got to meet him. She did hear some of his stories that he passed on to her dad and uncles and even her sister. One of Roberta's favorites is a Christmas story her dad passed on to her. When she thinks of this story, she says a special thanks to Grandpa Louis, whom she never met, but who brings her so much joy through his stories.

The Carson family lived somewhere in north central Kentucky when Grandpa Simpson heard about them. Phillip Carson and his wife, Margie, had one young daughter named Madie. Christmas was coming, and little Madie had decided what she wanted for her special present.

"I want a little white puppy," she told her parents. "Will you please get one for me?"

"I don't know," said her mother. "I don't know who might have one."

There were no pet stores then in that part of the country, so the parents couldn't go down and put in an order.

"I think the Wades' dog just had a litter of pups," said her father. "I don't know if they have a white one or not. We could go over and take a look."

"You have to promise to take care of it if we get one," her mother told her.

"Oh, I will! I promise!" said Madie.

"And don't get your hopes up until we find out," said her father. "Even if they have a white puppy, Mr. Wade might have already promised it to someone else."

"Could we go tomorrow?" asked Madie. "It wouldn't take long. They just live a mile or so down the road."

"All right," her father said. "We'll go in the morning."

Madie hardly slept that night, and she was the first one up in the morning. She gulped her breakfast and milk and waited impatiently for her parents to finish. Finally, they were in the wagon headed down the road.

They received good news when they arrived at the Wades. There was one white pup in the litter.

"You are welcome to him," said Mr. Wade, "but he's a little young to leave his momma right now. He will be the right age about Christmas."

"I'll come pick him up on Christmas Eve," said Mr. Carson.

Madie didn't want to leave the puppy behind, but she knew it was for the best.

"He could tell that he was going to be my puppy," she said. "I could just feel it!"

Madie used the time while she waited for Christmas to fix the puppy a bed in a large basket. She used one of her doll quilts to line the bed so it would be comfortable for her new puppy when he arrived.

Just before Christmas, Phillip Carson and Madie went into the woods and cut a perfect Christmas tree. That night, Margie, Phillip, and Madie decorated the tree with homemade ornaments, ropes made out of paper, and cotton for snow. They popped corn and laughed together as they prepared for their favorite holiday of the year. This Christmas at the Carsons' home was not to be as happy as they thought, though.

Four days before Christmas, Phillip took the wagon and horses into town for some last-minute baking supplies. While he was in town, a heavy snow mixed with sleet began to fall. As he neared his home, he could feel that the roads were already slick. Suddenly a small animal rushed through the bushes and startled the horses. They reared in the air and tried to run, but the wagon slid into a ditch by the side of the road. As Phillip climbed out of the wagon, the horses lunged forward and knocked him against the bank. His head hit a rock, and he never regained consciousness.

Instead of a Christmas party at the Carson home, there was a wake. When the funeral was over and the neighbors had come and gone, Margie and Madie were left alone with their grief. That night was Christmas Eve, but they did not feel like celebrating.

"I wish Daddy had brought my puppy home before he died," Madie said.

"I'm sorry," her mom told her. "I guess it wasn't meant to be."

"But Daddy promised," said Madie. "I think he will find

a way. The dead can walk on Christmas Eve, Momma. Maybe he will bring my puppy home."

"That's not going to happen," Margie told her little daughter. "Come, let's say our prayers and go to bed."

When Madie woke on Christmas morning, she thought at first that it was like any other Christmas. Then she realized that this year, her dad would not be there. Her mother was still asleep, but Madie lay there wide awake, listening. Something had caught her attention. Something was at the door. She heard scratching and heard a tiny yelp. It sounded like a puppy!

"Momma! Momma! Wake up!" she called out. "Something is at the door. Hurry!"

She and her mom threw the covers back on their beds and ran to the door. Madie opened it and saw a small white puppy standing there on the porch, looking up at her.

"Daddy brought my puppy!" she said. "Look, Momma! He brought it just like he said!"

"I'd like to think that, Madie, but I am sure Mr. Wade brought it by for you," her mom said.

"Mr. Wade would have left tracks!" said Madie.

"Well, bring it in and we'll find out later," Margie told her daughter. "What are you going to name it?"

"Christmas," said Madie. "I'm going to call it Christmas!"

A few days after Christmas Day, Madie and her mother went to thank Mr. Wade for bringing the puppy by on Christmas morning.

"I didn't!" he said. "The pup was simply gone when I

went out in the morning. It was too young to find its way to your house by itself. It's a mystery to me!"

It was a mystery nobody ever solved. Could the puppy have come by itself? If so, where were the tiny tracks? Could Phillip Carson have risen from his grave and brought his little daughter the Christmas gift he had promised her? Madie believed the latter explanation.

She and Christmas had many happy years together. On Christmas Eve, she always said a special thanks to her father. She knew that he would be close to her forever, and so would Christmas.

Christmas Message for Mother

Roberta tells this story about a family that lived near her when she was a girl.

My older sister, Fatima, and I always wished for a brother, but we never had one. I have chosen to include Simpson in my professional name in order to carry on the family name. We were lucky, though, to live by a family that had only three boys, so they became our big brothers.

Fatima was closer to the boys than I was because they were her age; I was ten years younger than Fatima. When the oldest boy, Fred, was killed in an automobile accident, we were as heartbroken as we would have been if he had been our real brother.

Fred's family was soon faced with another tragedy. The

father died of a heart problem. With him gone, the middle son, Carl, and the youngest son, Clyde, told their mother, Anna, that they could not run the farm. They had military careers in mind. Carl joined the Marines, and Clyde joined the Army.

Anna remained on the farm alone, but the boys wrote faithfully to her. She looked forward to the coming of the mail because it usually brought a letter from one of them.

Then, suddenly, the letters from Clyde stopped coming. Days, and then weeks, passed with no word. Anna began to think the worst.

It was close to Christmas, and Anna missed her family very much. Carl wrote, trying to encourage her to believe Clyde was all right, but she knew in her heart that he wasn't.

My sister Fatima had married and moved away by then, but she and her husband came home for Christmas. She visited Anna as soon as she arrived home and learned that Clyde hadn't written.

"I have lost a husband and a son," Anna said to Fatima. "I can't lose another boy."

"I am sure you will hear soon," Fatima told her.

"I prayed to hear something about him by Christmas, but tomorrow is Christmas Day and there won't be any mail," said Anna.

Fatima felt sad for Anna, but she was right. No mail ran on Christmas, and they had no phone. Anna would just have to wait and hope for news.

Fatima fell asleep on Christmas Eve thinking about

Anna. In the early morning hours, she had a vivid dream. In her dream, she heard someone call to her from outside. She looked out the window and saw Fred, looking as alive as he had been before the car wreck.

"Come in!" said Fatima, happy to see him. She knew Fred was dead, yet it seemed natural to be talking to him.

"I can't come inside," Fred told her, "but I have come to give you a message for Mom. Tell her that Clyde is okay. He has been wounded and has been in a hospital. He wasn't able to write for a while, but she will get a letter from him next week."

And then he was gone.

The dream woke Fatima, and it was so real that she actually got up and looked outside. Like the Christmas carol, it was truly a silent night. She knew the message was real, though.

After breakfast on Christmas morning, Fatima hurried down to Anna's house.

"Clyde's okay!" she told Anna. "You'll hear next week."

"How do you know that?" asked Anna. "Who told you?"

"Fred told me to give you the message," Fatima said. "I know it's the truth."

Fatima then told Anna everything she could remember about the dream. It wasn't real news, but it was real enough to give Anna hope. Hope was the gift she needed that Christmas.

The next week, there was indeed a letter in the mail from Clyde. But Anna already knew what he had written.

In the letter, he said that he had been injured and could not write to her while he was in the hospital. He was okay now and would be coming home on a furlough.

Fatima never forgot that Christmas Eve visit from Fred. Was it only a dream? Or had he somehow crossed the bridge between life and death to bring a message his mother so badly needed?

The Greatest Gift

Lonnie remembers this story about his uncle one Christmas.

Uncle Lilburn Brown came to visit us once a few weeks before Christmas. We were all excited about what we hoped Santa would leave us under the tree that year. I thought a bicycle would be the greatest gift any boy could get, and my brothers and sisters chimed in with their wishes for other material things.

"Those are all good things," Uncle Lilburn agreed, "but I heard about something that happened last Christmas that made me change my mind about what kind of gifts are important for Christmas."

"What's better than a bicycle?" I asked.

"Let me tell you what happened," he said, "and you can decide for yourself."

We gathered close as he told us this story.

"I was over in Wayne County last December visiting some relatives," he told us.

"I got there after Christmas, and they were still in awe of what had happened to their neighbors.

"The family of four lived down the road from them and, like most of their neighbors, they were looking forward to Christmas. The father and mother did not have expensive gifts, but there was a doll for the little girl and a BB gun for the little boy. Of course, there would be sticks of peppermint candy and an orange in their stockings.

"Christmas was a week and a half away when a snowstorm hit, bringing ice and freezing rain. The family had finished supper and were sitting around the woodstove when they heard the animals acting up in the barn. The father put on his coat to go see what was causing the ruckus.

"'I'll be back in a few minutes,' he told his family, and walked out into the storm.

"The children sat close to their mother as she read them a Christmas story. Outside, the wind whipped the snow around, but inside all was calm.

"The father braced himself against the wind and stepped off the porch. It was slicker than he realized, and his feet flew out from under him. He landed on the graveled path that led to the barn. He hit his head in the fall, and everything went black for a few minutes.

"When the darkness passed and he could see again, he tried to get up; but the bump on his head had left him dizzy. He called out, but the wind carried his voice away. He had to get his wife's attention some other way.

"He managed to dislodge some of the pieces of gravel

from the snow, and he began throwing them against the living room window one by one.

"His wife didn't notice at first because she was involved in reading, but then she realized that something was hitting the window besides sleet. She also realized that her husband had been gone for several minutes. He should have been back already.

"She opened the door and saw him on the ground. With the help of her son, she pulled him inside and got him to bed. She gave him hot soup and tea, but he continued to shiver and his fever continued to climb. Pneumonia was inevitable. By the end of the week, he was gone.

"Gone was the joy that had filled their hearts. Gone were their plans for a wonderful Christmas. Christmas carols fell on deaf ears, and grief filled their hearts. Neighbors helped as much as they could, but when the funeral was over they went back to their own homes.

"The children asked if their father would be home for Christmas, but the mother only shook her head as the tears rolled down her cheeks. They got ready for bed, but the mother, who had never had to take care of the fire at night, put extra wood in the stove before turning out the light. It was now Christmas Eve, but the mother and children were totally exhausted by death and grief.

"About midnight, the mother woke to a strange plinking sound against the window. The children woke a minute later. The sounds were just like the sounds their father had made the night he fell outside.

"Then the mother became aware of a roar from the flue. It was on fire! They had to get out of the house. The three pulled on their coats and ran outside. If they hadn't heard the sounds, they might not have awakened in time. What could have made those plinking sounds against the window? They looked under the window and saw a small pile of gravel there!

"By that time, the neighbors had seen the fire and called for help. The fire was put out and the house saved. The neighbors stood around, talking about how lucky the mother and children had been.

"The mother and her children smiled at each other because, unlike their neighbors, they knew it was not luck. Daddy had come home at Christmas and brought them the greatest gift of all—the gift of life!"

Gift of a Chime Child

A chime child is a child born when the clock is chiming midnight between Christmas Eve and Christmas Day. A chime child is said to be blessed with the gift of "second sight."

Roberta has a story about such a child. This is how she tells it.

Laurie, a distant cousin of mine on the Simpson side of the family, was a chime child. Her ability came in handy one Christmas when she was visiting us.

My Great-Great-Grandmother Alley had a special gift,

too. Her specialty was working with herbs. Many people called on her when a doctor was not available. The country doctor had a large territory to cover, since there was no hospital where patients could be centrally located. When he was away, Grandma Alley (everybody called her that because of the "greats" in front of her name) did what she could to help the sick.

She wrote down all her remedies in a large notebook. She included information about what each herb was good for. She also grew her own herbs and dried them for use in the winter. She kept her ample supply in a cabinet, and she kept her notebook on a little table near her bed. After she died, the family left the herbs in the cabinet and the notebook where she left it.

One Christmas after Grandma Alley died, Laurie and her family came to visit. My dad, Tom Simpson, was a young boy then. He said that during the visit, Laurie's younger brother Bobby came down with a fever. That was a scary thing back then. People feared scarlet fever, typhoid fever, and the flu. The family had no idea what was wrong with Bobby, and they worried when his fever did not respond to any of their home treatments.

They sent for the doctor, but he had gone to visit his daughter's family for Christmas. Bobby was getting worse, and nobody knew what to do to help him.

"Why don't you ask Grandma Alley what to do?" asked Laurie.

"Honey," said her mother, "Grandma Alley is dead. She isn't here."

"Yes, she is!" exclaimed Laurie. "She's standing by Bobby's bed!"

Remembering that chime children can see ghosts, her mother said, "Ask her what medicine we should give Bobby."

Laurie seemed to be listening to someone speaking directly to her.

Then she said, "Okay! Thanks, Grandma Alley."

Laurie turned to the family.

"She says to look at her notebook and then go to the cabinet. The jar with the herb you need will be pulled out a little bit in front of the other jars. Use the herb to make a tea for Bobby."

They turned to look at the notebook, and they were amazed to see that it lay open on the table. They checked the notes and found the herb in the cabinet. Then his mom made him some of the herb tea.

Within the hour, Bobby's fever broke and he slept peacefully. The whole family was relieved and amazed that Laurie, the chime child, had used her gift to heal him.

My dad said that after that, every time someone in the family got sick, they would find Grandma Alley's notebook open to the remedy they needed. When they moved away from the old home place, the notebook disappeared. There were more doctors then. Maybe Grandma Alley thought she was no longer needed.

Christmas Shopper

Years ago, we were at a book fair in Owensboro. One of the nicest things about book fairs is that people stop by to chat and tell us stories. One woman stopped by our table to look at our books and mentioned that books make good Christmas gifts.

She and Roberta started talking about the wisdom of shopping early.

"I have most of my shopping done by the end of summer," said Roberta. "That way, I can take my time wrapping the gifts while I listen to Christmas carols. It also takes the pressure off if I just want to go to the mall and enjoy all the decorations and music. I even find a last-minute gift sometimes, but there is no pressure to shop for all the people on my list."

"I used to put off shopping until the last minute, but I don't do that now," said the woman. "I make a point of being inside my house, safe and warm on Christmas Eve. I had an experience once that changed my routine."

"What happened?" Lonnie asked.

"You might not believe me," she said. "It was strange."

Of course, that made us want to hear her story more than ever, so we encouraged her to tell us.

"The stranger, the better!" Roberta said.

"When my husband was alive," the woman said, "I always put off my shopping until the last minute. He was good-natured about it and went along with me. He said it wasn't safe for a woman to shop at night alone. I told him that was silly, but he warned me every year that it was dangerous.

"I certainly had no safety concerns with him along. He was a tall man, and he always wore his black hat and overcoat on our shopping sprees. It gave him a look of somebody who shouldn't be messed with. I never felt threatened by anyone when he was with me.

"Then, a few years ago, my husband was killed in a car accident. I was devastated. How could I get in the holiday spirit with him gone? I had no intention of celebrating Christmas that year, so I gave no thought to shopping at all. I told my family that I wanted a quiet day at home alone.

"Then my sister called me late on Christmas Eve afternoon. She and her husband had decided to drive to Owensboro very early Christmas morning to spend the day with me. She didn't think I should be alone on such a special holiday. Christmas was for families! she said. But I knew I would feel alone without my husband regardless of who else was there.

"I immediately set about cleaning the house. When I finished with that chore, I was in the kitchen, planning my menu for Christmas dinner, when I suddenly realized I had bought no gifts for my guests. I knew they would come loaded down with presents, so I would have to get them something. It was about 9:45 at night, and I remembered that there was one department store that was going to be open until midnight on Christmas Eve.

"I grabbed my coat and drove to the store. I had no

idea of what to get, so I just walked up and down the aisles, looking for possible gifts. The decorations and music meant nothing to me. My husband was gone, and I was just going through the motions of living.

"After walking up and down a couple of aisles, I noticed a man who seemed to be following me. When I looked at him, he picked up a packaged shirt without really looking at it and put it back down. I didn't like the way he was looking at me, but then I realized he might be a security guard watching for shoplifters. I put him out of my mind and bought some presents.

"When I looked around the store, the man I had seen earlier was nowhere in sight. I felt relieved that he had gone. I had just let my imagination run away with me. He probably hadn't been following me at all.

"It was nearing midnight as I left the store. A few people left at the same time, but they went in a different direction than where I had parked my car. I heard the voices of other people coming out of the store, but I didn't look back. I only wanted to get to my car and drive home.

"As I walked down the street, I passed other stores that were closed. I began to feel uneasy. And then I saw something move in the alley entrance. The man I'd noticed in the store was waiting in the shadows!

"I stopped, frozen by fear, as he charged toward me. I clutched my purse and packages and waited for the worst. I knew I was in grave danger, but I couldn't move. I saw the flash of a knife blade under the streetlight.

"Then the man stopped! I could see his face in the streetlight, and he was clearly frightened. He wasn't looking at me now. He was focused on something behind me. I thought maybe the store's security officer had come outside.

"Suddenly, my fear released me and I started screaming.

"'Help! Somebody help me, please!'

"People came running. Other customers had seen the whole thing as they were leaving the store. I thanked them for scaring him away.

"One lady said, 'We didn't do anything, honey. It was the man walking behind you that scared him off."

"'What man?' I asked her.

"She looked surprised that I asked the question. 'Why, the man in the black hat and overcoat. He was right behind you. He started after that creep and chased him away. We never saw him again. I hope he caught the guy!'

"She and some of the others helped me to my car and I drove away, stunned by what had happened. The lady had described my husband perfectly in the black hat and overcoat. I had always heard that the dead could walk on Christmas Eve. Had my dead husband come back to save me after I disregarded his warning about shopping alone? I felt like he had.

"I never felt alone after that night. But I made a point to shop early from then on. I even bought extra gifts in case I needed some unexpectedly!"

New Year's Eve and New Year's Day

Since the 1900s, it has become customary to celebrate New Year's Eve on December 31 and ring in the New Year.

Many celebrate with parties, champagne, and a kiss at midnight. They make New Year's resolutions and sing "Auld Lang Syne." Fireworks and music accompany the stroke of midnight, ushering in the New Year.

Some people, like us, prefer a quiet evening at home watching the ball come down in Times Square, New York.

New Year's Day is celebrated in different ways all over the world, but everywhere it represents a new beginning.

In the United States, it is traditional to spend the day with loved ones, eating good food and watching parades and football.

Since it is a time for change, it is a time that might lure spirits to this side to visit.

New Year's Ghost

Roberta has a story about her Great-Uncle Charles. She tells it this way.

When I was growing up, we did not have big New Year's Eve parties, and we had no TV to watch the ball come down in Times Square. We did not toast the New Year with champagne or kiss each other at midnight. Mostly, we looked forward to our traditional southern New Year's Day dinner of cornbread, black-eyed peas for luck, cabbage or greens (turnip, collard, or mustard) for money, baked sweet potatoes for love, and ham or pork roast for health.

My great-uncle, Charles, was usually at our house on New Year's Eve. After his wife died, Uncle Charles became a "floater." That meant that he floated from one relative to another, staying two or three months at each place before moving on. He usually came to our house sometime around Thanksgiving and stayed until after the New Year.

Great-Uncle Charles had some beliefs that he observed on New Year's Eve. He put a coin outside the door on New Year's Eve because he thought it would bring prosperity for the coming year, and he insisted that all the outside doors be left open at midnight to let the old year out and the new year in unimpeded. I never noticed any increased prosperity from the coin, but, since he always left it there, I had no way of knowing if we'd have a bad year without his practice of putting it out. There was no means of comparison.

Leaving the coin outside caused no problem, but opening the doors in winter was a most uncomfortable thing to do! Our house was heated by a fireplace and a woodstove in the kitchen. We did not welcome cold air from the outside when we were gathered around the fireplace trying to keep warm. Great-Uncle Charles ignored our complaints and said he knew we came from sturdier stock.

"You shouldn't cringe and shiver at a little cold," he said. "It's good for you!"

It didn't seem good for some of us. As soon as the clock struck midnight, my sister and I waited for Great-Uncle Charles to signal that it was okay to race to the doors and close them.

Then one fall, Great-Uncle Charles didn't come for his usual visit. His brother sent word to Grandma Simpson at the end of August that Charles wasn't feeling well. His heart was bothering him, but there weren't many treatments for heart conditions back then. He died in early September.

Thanksgiving and Christmas were sad without him, but both holidays were uneventful. Then New Year's Eve came, and we thought of Great-Uncle Charles. As much as we loved him, we had no intention of carrying on his New Year's traditions.

It was a still winter night. No wind was howling to spook us as we sat around the fireplace, telling stories and wondering what the New Year might bring. We listened to the tick-tock of the clock and waited.

The clock's hands reached one minute before midnight.

Suddenly, all the outside doors blew open! For a minute, we sat there stunned, and then the clock began to strike. Dad told my sister and me to go close the doors. We looked out on a peaceful yard and garden. No wind was blowing, not even a breeze. There was no natural force operating here.

We smiled and welcomed what we knew would be a happy year. After all, Great-Uncle Charles had come back to visit!

Vengeance

At one of our book signings, we were approached by a man who said his name was Moreland. He told us a tale of vengeance in western Kentucky. We thought it was typical of the kinds of tales we were told where we grew up: a tale of murder and revenge.

It was the early 1900s. Jessica and Grady had been married several years, and the bloom had faded from their romance. They argued day and night about everything that came to their minds.

"Nothing I do for you is ever good enough!" yelled Jessica.

"You are so right!" Grady yelled back. "I think I am going to find someone to replace you!"

"Nobody would have you," said Jessica. "But if you did fool someone, I assure you I would never let them have any peace in my house!"

On and on it went, day after day. Fortunately, Jessica

and Grady had no close neighbors to hear their fighting, so people thought they were a happy couple. Both managed to put up a good front in public.

New Year's Eve drew near, and Jessica and Grady were invited to a party at a neighbor's house. Grady began to make a New Year's resolution right then to change his life. He decided that Jessica had to be eliminated. The party would be a good place to check out new prospects.

Jessica saw it as a chance to buy a new dress and socialize, too. The couple called a temporary truce and left for the party.

Grady and Jessica had no car, so they decided to walk to the party instead of hitching up the buggy. There was one stretch of road that was dangerous because there was a sheer drop-off. Neither admitted it to the other, but both were nervous when they passed that section of the road.

The party was in full swing when they arrived. Everyone was dressed up, and many were dancing to music by local musicians. Food and wine were plentiful, and the guests were enjoying both.

A cold rain set in, but only a few, including Jessica, noticed. She thought of the walk back home.

Grady made note of several new faces and made sure he introduced himself to each young lady as the evening passed. Jessica watched, but since they were in a large gathering, she held her tongue.

The hosts brought out champagne as midnight approached, and everyone toasted the New Year as the clock struck midnight. The rain stopped, but it had been heavy and left the ground muddy.

After listening to the loud revelry for a few minutes, Jessica went to find Grady. By that time, he was feeling the effects of the champagne and was in need of some fresh air. He didn't argue with Jessica when she suggested that they leave. He had accomplished what he had set out to do. He had met a fine-figured young lady who showed some interest in him. He could make no move tonight, but he left feeling certain they would meet again in more private circumstances. There was just one problem now: Jessica.

Though the rain had gone, the wind had picked up. Both Jessica and Grady pulled their coats tighter around themselves and walked a little faster. Jessica wished she had not worn new shoes. High heels were not suited for walking in mud.

The road narrowed as they came to the section with the drop-off. Grady moved behind Jessica as they reached the spot.

Do I dare? He wondered. *It would be so easy! Everyone would believe it was an accident!*

It was his only chance to court the new lady. He lunged forward and grabbed Jessica, pushing her toward the drop-off.

At first, Jessica fought and clung to Grady, but he was stronger. She wobbled on her high heels as she struggled.

"I'll have revenge!" she shouted, as he gave one final push that sent her over the edge, screaming.

Her body hit the ground below and the screaming stopped. Grady couldn't see Jessica's body in the dark. He waited a few minutes to see if he could hear anything. All was silent.

Grady turned and hurried back to the party. He burst through the door calling out, "Help! There's been an accident. Jessica has fallen over the drop-off."

The news ended the party and the search began. Searchers had to take the long road down around the hill to get to the bottom of the drop-off. It was daylight before they found Jessica's crumpled body. The pretty new shoes were all covered with mud.

"Those high heels are probably to blame. It looks like she slipped and fell, just like you said," one of the searchers said to Grady.

Jessica's death was ruled accidental, and Grady pretended to grieve. As soon as he thought he could get away with ending the grieving process, he began to call on the pretty lady, Stella, whom he had met at the New Year's Eve party.

The romance flourished, and soon Grady married Stella and brought her to the home he and Jessica had shared.

Right from the first, Stella was not happy.

"Grady," she said. "I have asked you over and over not to track mud into the kitchen. Look at the floor!"

There was no doubt that she was right about the mud all over the floor, but she was wrong to blame her husband. He said he didn't do it. As the days passed, it became an unpleasant issue between them.

One day, Grady examined the mud tracks closely and noticed that it looked as though a high-heeled shoe had carried the mud inside and then smeared it. He thought of Jessica's last threat.

That's impossible! There must be another explanation! he thought.

At the same time the mud made its appearance at Grady and Stella's house, reports started coming in from people who said they heard a woman screaming at the drop-off. A few swore that they saw the ghost of Jessica walking that section of road.

"That's nonsense," Grady said to Stella. "Things like that don't happen."

Stella became frightened. She now found the smeared mud all over the kitchen floor when Grady was not home. If Grady didn't bring it in, then who did? She became suspicious about Jessica's death. What if it hadn't been an accident? What if Grady had pushed her? If she failed to please him, thought Stella, would he do the same to her?

Finally, one day Stella waited until Grady was away from the house, then packed a bag and went home to her parents. She left a note for her husband saying she would not be back.

When Grady came home that day, he could not accept the contents of the note. He had to bring Stella back. He saddled his horse and rode down the road toward her parents' house to try to persuade her to come back to him.

He wasn't thinking about the road or the section with

the drop-off that he was approaching. He was intent on getting Stella back.

Suddenly, a shrill scream filled the air. Directly in front of him stood the ghost of Jessica! At the same time, Grady's horse reared and sent him flying through the air—right over the drop-off.

Another scream filled the air, but this time it was Grady's.

Jessica's revenge did not bring peace to the spirits of the restless twosome. Still at night, travelers hear the screams of a man and a woman at the drop-off. People who bought the house that Grady had owned complained of sometimes seeing mud on the kitchen floor and hearing the soft laugh of an unseen woman whispering, "Vengeance!"

Conclusion

Whether you are a believer in ghosts or not, we hope you enjoyed these stories as much as we enjoyed putting this collection together for you.

As you have seen, ghost stories are not just for Halloween. There are ghost stories for all year round. Storytelling is one of Kentucky's greatest traditions.

When you are thinking of gifts for holidays, remember that a printed book or an e-book would be nice. But a magical gift your loved ones will never forget is actually hearing a story!

Acknowledgments

The summer of 2014 was a sad one for us. Two of our dearest friends died in quick succession. We dedicate this book to Dwayne VanderEspt and Jerry Anderson in loving memory. They live on the other side now, but they also still live here in our hearts forever.

Dwayne died suddenly on June 24, 2014, at the age of sixty-four. We first got to know Dwayne several years ago as our computer technician, but he soon became a treasured friend. We acknowledged him in our earlier books because he gave us so much support in getting them ready for publication and in promoting them after publication. Besides making sure our computer was all right, he often checked to see if we were all right, too.

Dwayne loved the Beatles, guitars, music, people in general, and his family. He was dedicated to his work with computers, but most of all, he loved being a loving husband, father, son of Louise, grandfather, and friend.

Thank you, Dwayne, for giving us so much care and support, and thanks to the entire VanderEspt family for giving us the same, even in their time of sorrow. We feel certain Dwayne will be around for consultations from the other side.

Jerry died unexpectedly on July 11, 2014, at the age of seventy-five. The three of us grew up together in Russell Springs, Kentucky, and remained best friends through the years, regardless of where we went. The songs and stories about "all for one and one for all" described us perfectly. We considered ourselves as family and thought of Jerry's children as our nieces and nephews.

We were always so proud of Jerry's accomplishments. He served in the U.S. Air Force on special assignment in Okinawa, Japan. He made his home in Madison, Wisconsin, where he joined the City of Madison Fire Department in 1964. In 1986, he started the City of Madison Arson Squad, which he led until his retirement in 1996.

He loved fishing, bowling, golfing, hunting, and being with his family and friends. He always encouraged us in our writing. Thank you, Jerry, for all our precious times together, and thanks to the Anderson family for their love and support even in their own time of loss. You know, Jerry, that even death cannot keep us from being best friends forever. We know you are with us always.

Dwayne and Jerry, how blessed we were to have you in our lives!

Books are made by more than the words of the authors. We

have so many people to thank for helping us in our work that their names would make a book in themselves. Space limits us, but we do want to acknowledge those who have played major roles.

Thanks to Ashley Runyon, acquisitions editor at the University Press of Kentucky, who looked at the manuscript first and then passed it on to the right people. A special thanks to our copyeditor, Donna Bouvier, who always knows how things should be done. We appreciate all the suggestions.

Thanks to Robert W. Parker (Mr. Ghost Walker of Downtown Louisville Ghost Tours) and Thomas Freese (master storyteller and craftsman) who read the manuscript and gave us valuable insight and feedback. Both are authors of many books and were willing to give us expert advice.

Thanks to David VanderEspt, Dwayne's brother, who came to our rescue when we needed help with our computer. We appreciate your expert help more than we can say.

Thanks to Sharon Brown, who took us to many haunted locations to gather information and meet some ghosts.

Thanks to artist Jill Baker and poet Lee Pennington for their contributions; and to Salvador Doggie, who supervised us all.

Thanks to authors Irene Black and Nash Ford for guiding us to some ghostly locations in Russell County that we had not visited before.

Thanks to Pattie Filley, Lewis Brown, Carol Ferguson, and all the people in the past and present who told us stories that we have passed on to you.

Acknowledgments

Thanks to the board, the staff, and the editors of the University Press of Kentucky who helped this book come to life. We are forever grateful for your faith in our work.

And a special thanks to all of you who buy our books or come to hear us when we tell our stories!

About the Authors

Roberta Simpson Brown and Lonnie E. Brown were born in Russell Springs, Kentucky, near Lake Cumberland; they now live in Louisville. Their families were friends for generations, so Lonnie and Roberta share a common background of storytelling that flourished in rural south central Kentucky. Married since 1977, they enjoy reading, traveling, and learning about the paranormal. Lonnie is an accomplished golfer and musician. Roberta is a retired teacher who now works as a professional storyteller. Roberta and Lonnie coauthored *Spooky, Kooky Poems for Kids.* Lonnie is the author of *Stories You Won't Believe.* Roberta is the author of *The Walking Trees and Other Scary Stories, Queen of the Cold-Blooded Tales, Scared in School,* and *Lamplight Tales* and the coauthor of *Strains of Music* with her sister, the late Fatima Atchley.

www.ingramcontent.com/pod-product-compliance
Lightning Source LLC
Chambersburg PA
CBHW021356090426
42742CB00009B/873

* 9 7 8 0 8 1 3 1 6 5 5 5 4 *